TERROR ON WALL STREET

I0468377

GORDON EADE
KENNETH EADE

Times
Square
Publishing

Our society is so fragile, so dependent on the interworking of things to provide us with the goods and services that you don't need nuclear warfare to fragment us anymore than the Romans needed it to cause their eventual downfall.

— Gene Roddenberry

This book is dedicated to Becky, Gordon's wife and life partner. We all should be so lucky to be loved by such a person.

FOREWORD

It began very quietly with a few signals that I missed. "Where are my car keys?" and "I can't find my glasses." I have been told that next I will have difficulty remembering recently learned facts and the ability to acquire new information, and eventually, I will lose my writing ability. As my memory difficulties peak, I will lose awareness of recent experiences and events and have increasing episodes of urinary incontinence. Then I will begin to experience personality and behavior changes. In the final steps, I will lose the ability to speak and ultimately to control movements.

Finally, I will be unable to hold my head up or even walk. My wife, lover and companion will be physically and mentally spent nursing me in a futile battle against an unknown assailant for which there is no cure. Death follows. The whole process will take as little as two years or as long as eight. With effort I will be able to slow down the process. It's called Alzheimer's disease and I've got it."

– Gordon L. Eade

In 2011, my father was diagnosed with Alzheimer's disease. Shortly thereafter, he gave me the manuscript for this book and asked me to work on it for him. Since that time, I have written eight novels, all of which focus on important issues. I now have come back to this project – the work of a man who was a financial genius who was able to retire before he was 54 years old and live entirely off his investments. It carries the wealth of his knowledge about investing and the stock market, and is his first venture into writing fiction. His idea was to use metafiction to teach financial principles. It's not really my style, but that was his concept and I tried to respect that. The main characters are his creation. I have helped him with the story. He already doesn't remember writing it. I hope that you and he will enjoy reading it.

– Kenneth Eade

PROLOGUE

In 2007, at the peak of the economic bubble, the financial services sector had become a wealth creation machine, ballooning in size to the point that it captured profits equal to 40 percent of the total corporate profits of all companies in the United States. There were new financial products, including a new array of securities so complex that even many CEOs and Boards of Directors didn't understand them. These financial products were an ever-driving force of the nation's economy.

Employees of some of our largest investment banks earned bonuses of millions of dollars, taking risks that they either did not understand or didn't care about that destroyed our economy and those of other countries worldwide. It now appears that it will take many years to recover from the damage done to the economy.

Politicians have, for years, been using low cost housing schemes to gather votes. They have discovered in the last twenty years that guaranteeing housing loans is a cheap way to buy votes, unaware that, at some time in the future, these unwise loans would explode and destroy the economy.

The United States Congress has, for the last seventy years, been enamored with providing modern housing for the poor. These housing projects have proven to create neighborhoods that are filled with crime and occupied with families that are not functional. Congress just does not understand the economics of the highly complex economic system in this country. Providing low rent housing to the underprivileged and the poor does not improve the living standards of the poor – it just creates additional problems.

A similar condition has developed in pension provisions for workers who do not have defined benefit pension plans.

The government passed legislation that encouraged private employers to unload the risk of defined benefit pension plans and pass the risk to the worker, assuming that the average worker was qualified to manage a stock portfolio. Private industry now knows that even highly skilled managers are not qualified to manage stock portfolios. So, the risk was dumped on the worker, who delegated management of the portfolio to a stock broker, who is immune from most responsibility under current laws.

It is well known that defined pension plans have all but disappeared, except for those for government employees and union workers and those replaced by defined contribution plans, leaving the worker with the responsibility and the risk on his shoulders, a position he or she is not skilled enough to handle.

In addition, academics have known now for fifty years that the industry has been methodically cheating the public by charging the public for services that are worthless, as demonstrated by countless peer reviewed studies by academia and their students.

Recent developments in our financial system indicate that the country is experiencing a dramatic and sudden shock, the depth of will not be known until the recovery. This pending depression is quite different than the previous one in the 1930's in that today both consumers and industry are over leveraged. Financial institutions are also over leveraged with their exposure to default by derivative instruments, and it is well beyond their ability to withstand defaults of those instruments.

The techniques that were used in the 1930's to reset the economy will simply not work, and I believe that the financial experts will try but not succeed. In an economy that is over-leveraged to historic proportions, economic stimuli will not do the trick. Banks will stop loaning to customers unless they have excellent credit. Bank to bank loans will freeze up since no one will trust each other's financial strength. Businesses will lay off as many employees as needed to return to some level of profitability. We are a consumer based economy and, until consumers pay off some of their bank and credit card debts, it will be hard to get credit, and we can expect credit card interest rates to rise.

This tome has been written in the genre called metafiction, where I have used fictional characters to portray facts that will teach you how to invest and how to avoid the traps set by the clever brokers employed by Wall Street to transfer your money from your bank account to theirs.

My students and I will disclose all of the dirty little tricks that your broker uses to steal your money and show you how to avoid them. I will tell you the returns that you should receive over the long run that your portfolio should produce depending on the amount of risk you take. I will suggest the amount of risk that you should take.

We know that the average employee who invests in the stock market earns about one half of the returns that the market provides. The result will be that a large portion of the population will retire only to live on a diet of dog food or live with their children unless we do something about this problem.

My characters will advise you how to set up your portfolio so that you will maximize the opportunity to obtain the best return possible depending on the type of risk you take. You will learn how to set up your account to defer capital gains taxes until you start to cash in some of your stocks when you retire. You will learn how to fight back against Wall Street and to hurt them as they hurt you, your friends and neighbors.

I believe that I can, by writing a novel with fictional characters, teach you how to invest and what to expect when you take risk. Investing in stocks and bonds requires taking some risk. Without taking risk, you cannot accumulate sufficient funds to retire in the style that you deserve. On the other hand, it is impossible to select someone who can do this for you.

Listening to stories and reading stories is by no means a passive exercise. We thrust ourselves into stories as active participants by taking a role in what we read or hear. Studies by psychologists have shown that stories are the most effective form of human communication, more powerful than any other way of packaging information. Psychologists have determined that telling stories is the most efficient means of persuasion in everyday life – that is the most effective way of translating ideas into action. Reams of facts and data rarely cause us to take action, whereas in a story, the characters in the story can cause you to act in a manner intended by me, your author.

Stories must give the listener an emotional experience if they are to ignite the reader to action. By far, the most effective and efficient method way to do this is to use metaphor and analogy. These devices are key components in the way we think. When I describe things in a story I am creating imagery that engages you in multiple ways. The brain does not distinguish between a living image and an imagined one. This is the psychic lever that opens the brain to hard wire what you will learn and store in your mind. Most stories have a sympathetic hero and they are shaped by three critical elements – a challenge, a struggle, and some resolution. As you read, you know that the hero will solve and overcome the roadblocks that I have placed in his journey to an acceptable and realistic solution.

I have chosen this form of communication because Wall Street has convinced the majority of investors that it is possible, by using your skill, to select a portfolio of securities that will outperform the market. This false idea is so strong that it is virtually impossible to convince the man on the street that he cannot beat the market, and trying to do it is a sure path to a financial disaster.

You will learn that Wall Street experts themselves rarely beat the market using the vast resources at their disposal. It's a fact that the financial services industry spends billions of dollars annually to convince the public that their research and analysis the only way to achieve success in the stock market. In fact, the apparent success that some of these experts obtain are simply gifts from lady luck.

I will give you a list of things that you must not do if you are to survive the stock market's periodic drastic random moves. I will show you how Wall Street uses what they know about how your brain works when you sense euphoric messages that will cause you to react in a manner that is not in your best interest. All of this information will be presented in an interesting manner by fictional characters you will learn to love and trust.

I have been an investor in marketable securities for more than seventy five years. My portfolio contains over 14,000 domestic and foreign stocks and bonds in accordance with Modern Portfolio Theory. The compound annual return of this portfolio is greater than the weighted average of its component parts. Yes, I am saying that a properly designed portfolio of securities will earn more money with less risk than a basket of stocks selected without consideration of the risks of the individual components, adequate diversification and the effects that the individual components have on one another.

If your broker is not skilled in putting together a portfolio of stocks, then you will not receive a return commensurate with the risks taken. There are two types of professional financial advisors whom you can trust who know how to build a proper portfolio for you. They are a Registered Investment Advisor (RIA) and a Certified Financial Analyst (CFA). These experts have a fiduciary duty to select for you a portfolio of stocks and bonds that are suitable for your financial position.

Compare this responsibility with that of a stock broker who has no responsibility by law to recommend securities that meet your requirements. In fact, brokers will sell you those securities that earn them the highest commissions and/or those that reward them with paid vacations to beautiful locations. The Certified Financial Advisor has been tested to guarantee all aspects of your financial situation and should consider them in designing a portfolio to meet your needs at a risk that you can tolerate. You can be sure that a CFA has mastered the science of investing in marketable securities and has been tested to insure his qualifications are kept current. Compare this with a stock broker who has passed a series Seven test. I will venture a guess that he does not even know what the term "fiduciary duty" means.

Finally, I have listed a set of scams that are often used by unscrupulous stockbrokers and insurance salesman to separate you from your savings so you can immediately recognize what a friendly salesman is trying to sell you. I will show you actual scripts used by stock brokers. Scripts like this on have been crafted by experts who know how to convince you to take the desired action they want from you.

I will show you why the recent stock market meltdown occurred and just who was responsible, and how another event like the one we just experienced will happen again unless the recommendations I offer are not followed.

In addition, I have provided a list of books by authors who have vast experience advising investors and describing for the public how to invest. I hope you will enjoy my book and learn from the colorful characters, who will deliver a message that every investor should know in an interesting and exciting manner.

– Gordon L. Eade
   2012

CHAPTER ONE BLACK FRIDAY

November 27, 2020 was a day like any other day after any other Thanksgiving. The birds fluttered about in the trees and sang. Everyone who wasn't too tired or too hung over from their holiday stuffing were lining up outside the local stores to take advantage of the "Black Friday" sales. People who didn't have the day off and who were not going to the sales woke up, got dressed and went to work, grumbling all the while that the Friday after Thanksgiving should be a national holiday. The stock exchanges opened as usual for the short day of trading. There was no pre indication of the havoc that was to come, except to some who saw that something was coming, but they didn't know what it was. At the Chicago brokerage firm of J.C. Mortenson Securities, a stirring had begun.

"Bob, someone knows something."

"What the hell are you talking about?"

Bob Brammon, a salesman for J.C. Mortenson, rose up from his cubicle to look at his colleague, George Nabors, who was staring at his computer screen as if he had seen a ghost in it.

"Really, Bob. Someone's shorting transportation stocks – bigtime. And major retailers like Walmart."

Bob's eyes widened.

"What is it?"

"I don't know, but everyone's getting in on it, buying puts on stocks in both sectors. Energy stocks, too."

"Should we take some of the action? Might be a good play."

"I don't know. It looks really fishy. The market's only open half day today. I'd want to study it a bit longer before I'd recommend it."

"In today's market, a second could pass and you miss an opportunity. I'm going in, on my own account."

"I thought your professor said there were no deals in the stock market."

"They're aren't. But it looks like someone knows something is going to happen, and it's not going to be good. Everyone else must be piggybacking on that investor."

"Looks like way more than one investor. Well, whoever he is, he has a hell of a lot of buying power. Hey – don't you have class today?"

"No, we've got to be at a Congressional hearing next week. We're off today."

***

The local Walmart at Crossgate Commons in Albany, New York had opened the doors for its Black Friday sale on Thanksgiving Day at 6 p.m., and had stayed open through the next day for the rush of holiday shoppers seeking deals. The air was heavy, perhaps a warning of an early snowstorm, but that didn't stop the deal seekers. They dressed in their battle gear: winter coats and jackets, hats, gloves and mittens, and rushed to the store with their shopping lists, charge cards and contents of their piggy banks. Even the Salvation Army Santa Claus was up early, ringing his bell in front of the store as the busy shoppers rushed in to get the best buys, some throwing coins into his bucket as they hurried past him.

Sharon Wilkins circled the parking lot, looking for an available space for her white Toyota Prius. Black Friday was like a war, a war that started in the parking lot and continued in the free-for-all in the store. Every shopper, behind every shopping cart, was in competition with every other shopper for the best bargains. It was like a fisherman had thrown a bucket of chum into shark infested waters.

Sharon glided up and down each car infested aisle of the parking lot in frustration. Not only would she not get a space near the entrance, she would be lucky to get any space at all. Her little Chihuahua, Chinky, sensing her anxiety, gazed up at her where she was curled in a little ball on the passenger's seat and smacked her chops.

"Yes, Chinky, Mommy's mad. If Mommy doesn't find a parking space soon, she's going to miss out on all the bargains."

Sharon noticed an old lady, walking toward her. She rolled down her window, feeling the cold blast of fresh morning air, and waved at the woman.

"Are you leaving?"

The old lady cupped a hand to her ear.

"What?"

Damn it, you old bat, what do you imagine I would be asking you? Are you dumb and deaf?

Sharon tried again, this time louder. "Are you leaving?"

"Am I what?"

"Leaving! Are you leaving?"

"Yes."

Sharon put the Prius into a slow, silent crawl, as the old woman waddled down the aisle. She scanned the rows of cars, trying to guess which one may be the old crone's car. It has to be that one, she thought, focusing on a faded green 1970's style Cadillac.

Probably the original owners. Her and Mr. Old Fart.

The old woman seemed to slow down before reaching her car, like an airplane taxing to the gate, taking more agonizing seconds out of Sharon's shopping time. She made a fist and hit her steering wheel, avoiding the temptation to hit the horn instead.

Don't want to give the old witch a heart attack.

The old woman opened her door and popped open her trunk, which slowly creeped open. The frustration chewed away at Sharon's patience, as the lady slowly placed her bags in the trunk, and then began the long walk back to the driver's seat. Cars were piling up behind Sharon, who put her turn signal on to reserve her spot. Nobody was going to take that space but her.

She saw the brake lights flash as the ancient Cadillac fired up, blowing a plume of smoke out of its tailpipe.

Take your time. Shit, take all day!

The Cadillac slowly backed out of the space, making the slowest turn in history, and then lingered there for a while, probably just to frustrate Sharon.

Finally, Sharon slid into her spot in the packed parking lot, swept Chinky up in her arms, and began a fast walk to the store entrance. She knew that there wouldn't be any free carts at the front of the store, so she joined a long line of patrons at the cart return, waiting for exiting shoppers to give up their carts.

Finally, she had one of her own. She put Chinky in the child seat, right next to her purse, and pushed the cart into the store, preparing for battle.

At the entrance a retarded boy was repeating the phrase, "Happy holidays, welcome to Walmart," to the hordes of shoppers wheeling in, but when he saw Sharon, his eyes became bigger.

He put his hand forward like a traffic cop.

"Stop!"

"What?" Sharon was getting more and more angry. First the old bat and now this retard.

"Is that a service dog?"

Is he kidding?

"Yes, yes, this is my service dog."

The retarded boy smiled. "Welcome to Walmart. Happy holidays!"

The two-story megastore was decorated to the gills for the holidays, with fake green, red and gold garland, shiny tinsel and twinkling lights on every aisle, and Christmas music merrily played from every corner of the store, as hundreds of customers filled their baskets, and scores of others waited in the long checkout lines with their carts piled high, overflowing with groceries and gifts. Every register was open, with a cashier on duty, swiping bar codes, making their own musical contributions to the constant tintinnabulation of the jingle bells.

Sharon navigated the toy aisle, looking for red tags on the items that were on her list. A Star Wars XI battle kit for Tommy; a Barbie beauty salon for Jenny.

At exactly 10 a.m., a man ran into the middle of the crowded store. He was dressed like any other shopper, but looked somewhat strange. Nobody paid attention to him until he fell on his knees, put his hands over his head and then to the floor, as if he was exercising or praying.

What a weird man.

One of the store workers came up to him and put a hand on his shoulder. The man stood up. He was smiling, but his forehead was covered in sweat.

"Are you okay?"

The man did not answer the worker. Instead, he lifted his arms to above his head, screamed, "Allahu Akbar!," and ripped open his jacket. Sharon was nervous. He was acting too strangely. She quickly turned the other direction and pushed her cart as fast as she could. She was so scared, she was shivering.

The smiling man pulled a cord on his jacket, and blew himself up. The fiery blast ripped through the center of the store, sending shards of glass and chunks of debris ripping through Sharon, knocking her down and tearing her apart. It slashed through the store, killing ten more people and injuring forty others. There was a split second of silence after the blast, peppered with the moaning of the injured. Seconds later, hundreds of panicked people, supercharged with adrenalin and fear, simultaneously ran as fast as they could to the exits, creating a frantic stampede. The smaller ones and the younger ones simply fell under the feet of the raging crowd, which flowed with the force of a wild, roaring rapids, crushing the more unfortunate ones under their feet. The masse crashed through the glass entrance and spilled into the chaotic parking lot, leaving behind another 48 victims in its wake.

At exactly the same time, suicide bombers at the Walmart Supercenters on Park Plaza Drive in Manhattan, North Broadway Street in Chicago, Coral Way Shopping Center in Miami, Central Expressway in Dallas, Edgewater Drive in San Francisco, and Evans Avenue in Denver were hit, with comparable casualties, and bombers in trucks filled with explosives took out three of the company's major distribution centers. War had been declared on the American economy.

CHAPTER TWO TERROR ON WALL STREET

On everyone's lips among the brokers and salesmen at J.C. Mortenson were the terrorist attacks. How is anyone going to be safe? What is the president going to do? The tragic events had turned the usual dull roar at the office at J.C. Mortenson into a hysteria-driven explosion of conversation, mixed with guttural expressions of frustration, despair and grief. On the screen above their cubicles, the horror was playing and replaying itself out on videos, taken from the cell phones of survivors of the Walmart massacres. On the bottom of the screen, the ticker ran the bad financial news, adding a component of financial carnage to the damage.

"Whoa! George, look at those numbers!"

Transportation and grocery retail giants' stocks were dropping in real time.

"Transportation and retail stocks are tanking!"

"I told you someone knew something."

"Holy crap, George, it has to be insider trading on the terrorist attacks."

Dumbfounded, Bob stared at the screen, feeling serious pangs of regret that he had jumped on the bandwagon and was now profiting from the terrorist attacks. On the screen, a news announcer came on with an exclusive report:

This is Barry Schneer, reporting from New York. We've been showing you video feed from the terrorist attacks at Walmart stores across the country, which appear to have been co-ordinated. ISIS has claimed responsibility for the bombings, and the president has called it an attack on all humanity. She has vowed that the United States will make a swift and appropriate response. Walmart stock has been plummeting, and other stocks in the transportation and retail sectors are reporting sharp drops, which have begun a selling frenzy on the market.

"Red arrows all over the place!"

"Bob, look! Major banking stocks are dropping. JP Morgan, Citigroup, Bank of America..."

Stocks of the "too big to fail" banks are also dropping. JP-Morgan Chase is down ten points. Citigroup is down by five and Bank of America is down by four in the selloff.

The normally busy phones at the office rang double time in succession to the hundreds of callers who must have been in queue. And sell orders were racing through the J.C. Mortenson online website.

As the course of the short trading day played out, the tickertape was almost solidly red. Retail, transportation and bank stocks had lost over 50% of their value, representing trillions of dollars of shareholder wealth. Bob was fidgeting in his seat, watching the clock as he became more and more anxious about the banking news.

"I'm with B of A. I'd better cash out while I can!"

Panic has hit the markets, with investors liquidating positions in the major banks, grocery retailers and transportation.

"Dude, don't worry, Bank of America is one of the biggest banks in the world."

"That's a reason to worry, George."

***

When Bob got to the bank, the line was out the door and around the block. A bank manager came out to the sidewalk to settle the crowd of impatient, angry and worried customers.

"Does anyone have a straight deposit, no cash transaction?"

The growing crowd was restless and impatient. A man in the line raised his voice.

"We want our cash out, not in!"

This prompted murmurs of protest from all the waiting customers. The manager reacted with a nervous smile, kept walking down the sidewalk, and repeated her question to the rest of the people down the block.

"We've got limited cash here. We have to order it. There's a limit on cash withdrawals of $300 inside. The ATM machines are right on the side of the building if you don't want to wait in line."

One irate man in line pulled her by the elbow of her jacket, and got in her face.

"Since when is there a limit? It's my money, and I want it now!"

"I'm sorry, sir, but each branch holds just enough cash to satisfy our average daily needs. Don't worry. The bank has plenty of money. We just need to order it."

The crowd erupted with fervor.

"There's a longer line at the ATM than inside the bank!"

"We want our money!"

As the group became more restless, another manager emerged from the bank, with a security guard.

"Ladies and gentlemen, the bank is closing. If you need to make a transaction, please use the ATM machines on the side of the building. Please move away from the door so we can close it."

Instead of moving away from the door, the mass of people just crowded closer to it, pushing and shoving at each other, and yelling in protest.

"Closed? How can it be closed?"

"It's only 3 o'clock! The bank closes at 5!"

"I want to close my account!"

Bob was in the back of the line, which was a good thing because, at the front, the mob was pressing at the double doors with such pressure, it seemed they were about to break. There was no closing them as the line of people finally forced their way into the bank lobby like a rush of water through a floodgate.

Bob left the line, and went around the corner to the ATM machine, but the line there seemed as long as the one to get into the bank, so he crossed the street to the supermarket.

The store was packed with people, who were pulling things off the shelves as fast as they could and loading up their grocery carts with mountains of food and canned goods, as if everything was free instead of being marked up 100%. Bob waited in line at the small ATM machine in the lobby of the store. After about 15 minutes, he was at the front of at the machine, putting his card in and punching in his PIN number. The screen flashed a response to his withdrawal request of $300:

Withdrawal limit exceeded.

"What the hell?"

He flipped out his cell phone and went on the Internet to check his account.

404: error, page not found.

"Son of a..."

He pulled up the site for his online brokerage account and logged in.

Password error.

Bob Brammon had a few bucks saved at his bank and a modest securities account with his employer, but now all of it had disappeared into cyber space.

CHAPTER THREE OCCUPY CHICAGO

The news was bleak. The president had vowed to take military action, and promised that measures would be taken to keep shopping malls safe. But a second story was developing that struck another chord of terror in the minds of Americans and many others all over the world.

The stock exchanges took another dive right after the opening bell. By Monday afternoon, trading on the New York, American and NASDAQ exchanges had been suspended after a second record day of more historical losses. The Dow Jones industrial average had fallen over 28% in just one and a half days of trading – its largest drop in history. The FDIC announced that it had seized Bank of America, but assured depositors that their deposits were covered by FDIC insurance up to $250,000 per depositor. In the wake of the Bank of America failure, the Managing Director of the International Monetary Fund warned that the international financial system was on the brink of collapse, and that major international banks were at risk of failing because of losses on speculative asset-backed derivative contracts.

The banks had about $1 trillion in deposits and over $50 trillion in derivatives securities. The total derivatives market itself had been teetering around $800 trillion – over ten times the size of the world's economy.

In the streets, there was a more stark form of reality. None of these interest points or trading failures made any sense to the ordinary citizens. All they knew was that, all of a sudden, their money was gone and, to make matters worse, food and gas was becoming scarce, prices were going up and they had nothing to pay them with.

Food riots broke out as major chains like Walmart were besieged by their own customers, who trampled through the doors with the fervor of a thousand Black Fridays. When their ATM or charge cards were declined, they simply ran out of the store, en masse, with groceries and merchandise. Since the weekend, most supermarkets in major cities across the country had been picked clean by hoarders and looters, and their supplies had not been restocked, causing them to close. By Tuesday, Walmart had filed for chapter 11 protection.

There was a string of suicides at the Chicago Mercantile Exchange, and the top executives of every major bank, apparently not aware of the captain and ship principle, were packed inside their private jets with their golden parachutes on their way to Europe or other offshore destinations.

The warning signs had been there since the crash of 2008, but, after the initial shock, nothing had been done to correct the problem. Banks had been trading over $7 trillion in risky derivatives daily, as well as fixing interest rates and making bets on the rigged games. There was an ever-growing gap between the elite and all the rest of the people that had continued to develop even after the 2008 crash.

The Government had been spitting out statistics that the economy was in recovery, that unemployment was down, and that the stock market was in the middle of another historic bull run, which was actually just another huge bubble. Triggered by the terrorist attacks, that bubble had burst and financial experts all over the western world were trying to figure out how to put the economy back together again.

Carlos Rodriguez, a graduate student in economics at the University of Chicago, whose father was a well-to-do businessman in Mexico, was preparing for a trip to Washington, where he would be a member of a team of financial experts headed by his economics professor, Dr. Harry Mason, a Nobel laureate in economics. As he packed his suitcase, he noticed that the traffic in the city seemed to be louder than usual. Blaring sirens, the sounds of helicopters circling overhead and people screaming overpowered the normal ebb and flow din of downtown traffic he had always been used to.

When he looked out his window, he saw that the streets were jammed with people, as if the Macy's Thanksgiving Day Parade in New York had been transplanted to Chicago and re-routed down La Salle Street. There was a large crowd from "Occupy Chicago" outside the Federal Reserve building on 230 S. La Salle. Some were holding signs declaring, 'We are the 99 percent.' Others protested the bank closures, blaming the Government for the crash of the economy, and demanding access to their cash and government aid. More crowds were gathered outside the U.S. Bank building on La Salle, and the Bank of America branch on Adams, demanding they open their doors. The streets were filled with people, choking off traffic, all the way to the federal building on Jackson and Dearborn and probably well beyond Carlos' field of vision.

Carlos watched with disbelief, as SWAT vans and armored personnel carriers pulled up, and hordes of police streamed out of them like attacking ants, shooting tear gas into the crowd and pushing at them to disperse the protesters. The crowd fought back, throwing rocks and bottles, which crashed around the police and bounced off their clear polycarbonate shields.

In just a few days the city had turned into a war zone. It seemed that freedom of expression had run amuck, or had run as far as the Government would allow it to go.

CHAPTER FOUR EXODUS

It was like the beginning of the end of the world. "Hope for the best, but prepare for the worst." That's what the survival hawks had said, but everyone had always thought they were crazy. Now, she realized they were right as she watched the mobs of people looting in the streets of Chicago, smashing windows, breaking down doors, and the police standing by in their riot gear, doing nothing about it. The sky was already a hazy brownish grey, probably from all the fires. She could hear the fire engine sirens and had seen plumes of smoke from all over the city on her taxi ride from the University of Chicago.

Keep enough cash in case of emergency.

Even her economics professor, Harry Mason, who was a relatively conservative, "buy and hold" investor, had advised to keep cash just in case and to also have some hard assets in your portfolio.

Shirley Baxter, called "Snookie" by most of the people who knew her, looked out the window of the cab at the chaos outside that used to be the streets of Chicago. Some people were lugging huge bottles of water, some rolling shopping carts filled with food. Still more were stealing the spoils from each other. Suddenly, a rock hit the side of the cab with a loud clank, just missing the window, and Snookie ducked down.

"You don't want to go out there," said the cab driver, a rough and tough type with a pack of cigarettes rolled up in the sleeve of his T-shirt, revealing a purple tattoo.

"Will we make it?"

"Oh, you'll make it to the airport, alright. I don't know about your plane. Where are you headed?"

"Washington. I'm supposed to be in a group who's testifying before the Senate Finance Committee."

"Well you tell them for me that they've screwed everything up. Excuse my French, but there's no other way to say it."

The driver dodged a burning car.

Snookie, a graduate student at UChicago, where she was a candidate for a PhD in economics, was still a ways from 30 and, even on a day like this, she was looking fresh, clean and confident, and was dressed in style. She brushed her long auburn hair behind her ear and put her cell phone to it. No signal. There were rolling blackouts out all over the city. Probably out in the transmission towers as well. Or the whole system was run by the Internet, like everything else. She wasn't getting a 4G signal, either.

As the taxi pulled up to the United Airlines terminal at O'Hare, the entire airport police force seemed to be out and on alert. It was impossible to see the curb, due to the mass of people packed into the sidewalk with stacks of luggage piled to the cosmos. The cops were waving at all the cars, moving them along. Luckily she was in a taxi, which still had a special zone to drop her off.

"I'd help you in, darlin', but they're not going to let me stay here," said the driver as he pulled up into the taxi zone.

"That's okay, I'll make it."

She paid the driver the $55.20 on the meter, plus a $10 tip, but he handed it back to her.

"Maybe this stuff will be good in Washington. Here, it's just paper."

Snookie took back the cash, reluctantly. Despite her early years, she had amassed enough of it to be independent. The noise was deafening. The honking horns, people yelling, police sirens and bullhorns blazing seemed to be amplified ten times their normal sound. The crowds were piling against the entrances to the terminal like a pack of buzzing bees. The police had put up concrete barricades, but the people were squeezing up against them. She pushed and prodded her way through the throngs of humanity to the opening. None of this was a part of her daily routine, and it made her extremely nervous and on edge.

"Ticketed passengers only," said the cop who was blocking the only functioning door. He, and his partner next to him, looked like an astronaut or a superhero from a comic book in their riot gear: black helmets with visors, heavy boots, black flak jackets, and more padding on their shoulders and chests than NFL football players. Another two "robo cops" stood next to them. Snookie showed the police her flight reservation printout and was allowed to pass. It's a good thing she had printed it, because there was no way to show them an email on her phone. Snookie was always prepared, but not for something like this.

Inside the terminal, the chaos seemed more subdued. Noting that the self-service terminals were out, she took a place in the huge line that was growing in mass at the customer service counter. Ten years ago, there were triple the staff to handle all the customers. Now there were triple the customers, and a staff who only handled baggage drop-offs. Only the supervisors knew how to write a ticket or print out a boarding pass, and they were in short supply. One of them, a woman, about

45, with hair that seemed to be graying by the minute, stood up on a stool behind the counter and raised a bull horn.

"Ladies and gentlemen, may I have your attention please?" The bullhorn amplified her voice, and made it sound electronic.

"Due to power outages to air traffic control, all flights have been cancelled until further notice. Any tickets you now hold on a United flight will be honored as a credit against a future flight."

"Yeah, if there are any future flights," quipped the guy in line next to her. She reacted to his comment with a quizzical stare – essentially no reaction at all.

The mass of people erupted with questions.

"How are we going to get to Los Angeles?"

"Are there flights going out of other airports?"

"Can I get a refund on my ticket?"

"What about trains and buses?"

"Ladies and gentlemen, I can't answer all your questions as a group. If you would like to keep your place in line, we will be happy to answer all of your questions at the counter. Otherwise, you can check the updates on our website at United.com."

Snookie turned away, plowing through the mass of nervous and frustrated people. She felt stuffy and claustrophobic. She needed to get to Washington, and there was obviously nothing the airline could do to help her.

"Snookie!"

She heard someone calling her, from what seemed like far away. There can't be anyone else with that name. Then she saw him, coming toward her, weaving in and out of people, waving his hand. It was Ike Pendleton!

"Ike, thank God it's you!"

Ike smiled, and gave her a hug. He had given her a friendly hug before, but she had always felt cold and distant to him. This time, she felt vulnerable, not the usually strong Snookie he had known – the girl who always had all the answers. Ike was a little older than her, and had the same Economics professor at UChicago, where he was doing his thesis in neuroeconomics. They were both part of a team of 'whiz kids" led by Professor Mason, who was working with them on a class project to save the economy.

"I'm glad I found you here, Snook. I was just about to get my car and head off to D.C. The chances of getting a plane anytime soon don't look too good. Want to join me?"

"Yes, for sure. Where's your car?"

"In the parking lot. It was hell getting it here, but once we get out of the city, it should be easier going."

"I'm with you. Let's get out of here."

It proved to be just as difficult to get out of the building as it was to get in, due to the fact that most people were trying to enter, not leave the terminal. Ike grabbed Snookie's overnight bag and threw it on top of his own roller bag, then blazed a trail to the crowded opening, dragging her along. She seemed so scared and helpless – nothing like the girl he had known from his economics class. Ike pushed and shoved his way through the crowd like a linebacker, trailing the suitcases and Snookie behind him. He turned his head to her.

"I guess we're a little late on saving the world, aren't we? It's kind of like a living lab, showing neuroeconomics at work."

"It's exactly what Professor Mason was trying to prevent."

***

When they finally got to the parking garage, they had to take the stairs because the elevators were not working. When they reached the third floor, Ike pointed and said, "My car's right over...what the hell?"

Ike let go of the bags, turned to Snookie and said, "Wait for me here," and ran ahead. Two men were breaking into his brand new Lexus. One was working a slim jim into the window while the other stood impatiently by him.

"Get away from my car!" Ike screamed and charged toward them.

CHAPTER FIVE FORGOTTEN

Dr. Harry Mason lived in a townhome near the University. It was a nice neighborhood, close to Washington Park, which Harry claimed provided them with an ample supply of fresh oxygen. He and his wife, Jennifer, had selected the house so Harry could walk to and from his economics classes. Walking was often a therapy for Harry. It freed his mind from other things, and allowed it to wander freely and be more creative. At other times, it was a necessity.

Jennifer had put the final touches on their packing, and had slipped into the shower. Harry was going through his brief-case, and suddenly, he realized that he had left an essential part of his presentation back at his office, his home away from home. He knocked on the bathroom door.

"Dear, I'm afraid I've forgotten something at the office," Harry said in his cockney English accent.

"What did you say, Harry?"

"I said, I've forgotten something at the office. I'm going to go and fetch it."

"Just wait a few minutes, I'll go with you."

"No, it's okay. I can do it myself."

"Harry, please wait for me."

Harry raised his voice. "Jennifer, this is ridiculous. I'm not a child. I've done this walk thousands of times."

He grabbed his jacket and steamed out the door, slamming it, then felt instantly bad for his outburst.

As he walked to the campus, confusion ruled the usually orderly neighborhood. The storefront glass at the local minimarket had been broken, and there were smashed groceries and spilled milk all over the sidewalk in front of it. The store seemed abandoned, and Mr. Drucker, the owner, was nowhere to be seen.

He reached the gate of the University, which had been barricaded to incoming traffic. Harry approached the guard's booth.

"What's going on here, George?"

"Oh, hi, Professor Mason. Don't you see? All hell's broken loose. We're not letting anyone on campus unless they show a student or staff I.D."

"Is it safe?"

"On campus, of course. But out there, I don't know."

"Well, thanks, George."

Harry continued past the booth to his office. Sure enough, the folder with his presentation outline and corresponding index cards was sitting on his desk. He grumbled to himself as he slipped it into his briefcase.

How could I have forgotten the most important thing?

Harry looked around to make sure that there wasn't anything else he had forgotten, then locked up the office and left for home. He could hear sirens in the distance, and small particles of ash were falling, covering everything on campus like a fine layer of grey snow. He could see larger pieces of them wafting through the air toward the ground. The smoke had cut off the sun, making it appear as if it were later than it really was.

Harry waved to George at the security stand and turned left on S. Cottage Grove Avenue. The usually calm streets had become even more agitated since he had left home.

***

A group of teenaged boys bumped into Harry at the corner, knocking him slightly off balance.

"What are you waiting for, old man?"

"Yeah, the lights are on but nobody's home!"

They laughed as they passed Harry. He looked at them, startled, and then at the street light as they crossed. He realized that he must have blanked out while he was waiting for the signal to change. There was no telling how long he had been frozen there. As the signal turned red, he watched the pedestrian countdown timer and counted with it out loud.

"Twenty two, twenty one, twenty..."

Finally, the light turned green and Harry proceeded to cross the street. But, once he reached the corner of 60th and Cottage, he didn't know whether to go forward, to turn, and, if so, which way to turn. The dark sky seemed to spin around his head, and he broke into a cold sweat as panic set in. Okay, Harry, get a grip on yourself. Just ask directions. Directions – to your own house.

A group of students began to pass him.

"Excuse me, could you please tell me how to get to..."

One of the girls stopped and looked at Harry, waiting for him to finish his sentence.

"Where do you want to go?"

Harry opened his mouth to speak, but then realized he had forgotten his own address. The girl continued to stare at him, impatiently, smacking on her gum. She turned her head to her friends.

"Be right there, guys."

Harry thought and thought.

"Uh, Sixty-second Street. That's it."

But what number?

"It's just ahead, two blocks."

"Thanks."

Harry felt like an idiot, and now wished he had gone to the office with Jennifer. Great pills. Real miracle drug.

As he wandered along, wondering what his address was, everything began to appear strangely unfamiliar. The neighborhood just didn't look right. He approached a group of three young men, who were working on a car.

"Excuse me?"

"What do you want, grandpa?" This brought a chorus of laughter from the other two.

"Yeah, can't you see we're busy?"

The first guy pushed at Harry's shoulder.

"You got money, pops?"

"What?"

"I said, give me your money, old man."

He shoved Harry again. Harry lost his balance, but one of the others caught him and threw him back to the first thug. Then, it turned into a shoving match, using Harry as the ball. The first thug took Harry's briefcase.

"Is the money in here?"

He opened it and spilled the contents all over the street, swiping through them, looking for cash. Harry got on his knees, and began scooping up the index cards. Another one of the men kicked him, and he hit the pavement on his side. As he lay on the ground, they ruffled threw his pockets, took his wallet, and ran off.

They must have been trying to steal that car.

Harry stretched out on his back and lay on the pavement for a while until the sky stopped spinning, then struggled to get back on his knees to gather his papers. He slid the briefcase toward him and put the papers into it in random order as he scooped them up. He found his cell phone in the pocket of the case, but couldn't remember his phone number. He punched the telephone icon and dialed the last number in the memory.

"Harry?"

"Jen, honey. I've had a little trouble."

"Where are you, Harry?"

"South Cottage Avenue, near the campus."

"I'll be right there. Don't move."

CHAPTER SIX THE WHIZ KIDS

The door to the lecture hall opened, temporarily startling the group already seated in the auditorium, and in walked Shirley Baxter, dressed to impress, which was her habitude, her hair done in an upsweep style. She walked slowly through the corridor, pausing to look at the credentials and awards collected by the professor over the last fifty years, including his Nobel Prize in Economics and a page from his PhD thesis showing a mathematical proof, the basis of Modern Portfolio Theory, which Professor Mason was known for.

Ike Pendleton nudged Carlos Rodriguez, "Look at that girl. She's a knockout, isn't she?"

"Be careful Ike, you're looking at a bomb ready to go off any minute now. Shirley's a genuine genius, who knows about everything and can instantly retrieve every bit of knowledge buried in her brain with awesome precision."

"And just how do you know that?"

"We spent some time together last summer in my father's home town in Mexico. She's a very exciting creature –just about everything you'd want – beauty, charm, sex appeal, and money."

"Money?"

"Don't ask, cuz I don't know. Didn't ask her. I've got a deal with the manager of the local hotel in San Miguel de Allende. He's always on the lookout for chicks that I may like to meet."

"Nice. And she was one of them?"

"Yeah. One evening, he introduces her to me, and she tells me to call her 'Snookie."

"Snookie?"

"Yeah, that's her nickname. I ask her, 'what brings you to our little city?' and she says, 'I've enrolled at University of Chicago to get my PhD in Economics, and I want to use your town as a laboratory for my thesis.' Imagine that! I spent three weeks helping her with her project, and we agreed to meet up in the fall, here."

"So you were one of her lab rats, huh?"

Carlos laughed.

"So what happened between you two?"

"Nothing. Dude, she's untouchable. All work and no play."

Snookie stopped, with finger in cheek, to examine the professor's mathematical proof, as if she had discovered some flaw in the mathematics. As she did, Professor Harry Mason entered the room. Harry was somewhere north of 70, but nowhere near retirement age. His cockney accent betrayed the fact that he had transplanted himself from his native Britain in the 1970's.

Harry was a tall, lean man, well-liked by his students. He delivered lectures in a clear and straightforward manner, and often stepped up to the blackboard to diagram a concept, to prove an assumption or to clarify an issue. All of his students were impressed with his demeanor, his delivery, and an attitude that revealed a dedication to education. They seemed to both love and fear him. When he sensed a student was not working up to his or her potential, he would burst forth with a raging statement, in his cockney drawl, which always instilled both fear and motivation.

Harry cast a powerful figure, dressed in his favorite sports coat, a hunting jacket with leather patches on the sleeves at the elbows, which gave the impression that he would be going on a fox hunt right after class adjourned, when actually he would be heading home for a late breakfast.

He had hand selected every one of the students for this special economics workshop, and Snookie was the one who had most fascinated him. He was most impressed by her prodigious memory and the impeccable records from all of the educational institutions she had attended in the past. He admired how she had turned down financial aid from all of them, stating that she had the money to pay for her education and that she didn't want to take from others who needed help.

When he had quizzed her about the source of her funds she told him that, with her earnings, she had invested in the stock market and had been fortunate in selecting the best system to use and was, in addition, very lucky that the market had been in a strong upward trend.

This was the first time the professor noticed that her character had changed from when they first met. Could it be he was witnessing a drama and that she was acting out every scene as appropriate to the audience and the occasion? There was something about the way she walked, her demeanor, that reminded him of someone, somewhere, whom he had once known or met. He thought, This is going to be a very interesting and exciting semester, but he was in no way prepared for the events that would unfold in the very near future.

"Good morning, Ms. Baxter," said Harry, with a smile. Snookie turned to him. "Good morning, professor."

"You have a question about my mathematical proof?"

"No." She turned back and went to find a seat in the first row.

No? Then why were you staring at it so strangely?

Harry shrugged it off and proceeded to the stage. The room was dressed in his personality. On the far wall was a stained glass window, depicting a meadow populated with deer and elk. One could feel, with some imagination, the breeze in the trees, smell the odor of the morning dew on the meadow grasses and hear the mating calls of the elk.

The walls and ceiling of the room were paneled with rare exotic woods selected by old world craftsmen. There were bookcases on both walls on either side of the hall. They contained bound copies of the Economist magazine and The Journal of Finance going back many years. In the corner of the room there was a piano whose keys played all on their own when you fed it quarters.

"Good morning, everyone, and welcome to Economics Workshop."

Everyone greeted the professor, but they all seemed to have an eye on Snookie, who slid into a seat next to Ike Pendleton and Carlos Rodriguez.

Carlos was a very handsome man, obviously from a wealthy family, with impeccable manners and grace. He was dressed in a silk leisure suit with expensive accessories and was wearing a very large diamond ring.

"You are all here today for various reasons, one of which is to earn a doctorate in economics. I am going to take that journey with you, but I'm going to ask you to work and work hard. As Dorothy said to little Toto in The Wizard of Oz, we're not in Kansas anymore and it will become evident shortly why I say that."

Ike whispered to Carlos. "He kind of looks like the Wizard." Carlos snorted, and Snookie gave him an irritated look.

"I can see some of you know each other already, so let's get the introductions over with, shall we? Mr. Rodriguez, you start. What do you hope to accomplish this year at UChicago?"

"Me?" Carlos swallowed his smile.

"Is there another Carlos Roridguez in the room?"

Ike snickered.

"You're next, Mr. Pendleton. Stand up, Mr. Rodriguez."

Carlos rose from his seat and looked around the room, tentatively. "I'm doing my project on the differences between capitalistic systems and socialist systems, and how to emphasize the advantages and minimize the problems to economies within the two systems."

"Thank you, Mr. Rodriguez. You can sit down now. Mr. Pendleton?"

Ike stood as if to give a speech.

"I specialize in neuroeconomics and I intend to do original research on how and why investors in the stock market appear to act irrationally and not in their best economic interests. I believe that, at times, they don't make rational decisions and that those decisions are influenced by Wall Street propaganda to their determent. I'm conducting experiments in my laboratory here on campus with rats, birds, rabbits, primates and other mammals to determine how they handle risk and why. I'd like to invite all of you to my research laboratory. I've got a couple of horses there that always need some exercise that you're welcome to ride any time."

Snookie looked at Ike, puzzled at what possible good it would be for an economist to study birds and rabbits.

"I'm sure we'll all take you up on your offer, Mr. Pendleton. I, for one, am fascinated with what rats and horses may have to do with the economy. Mr. Brammon, how about you?"

Bob Brammon specialized in quantitative analysis and was working on a high speed computer trading project.

"I'm doing my thesis on trading systems using super high-speed computers to maximize profits from minute price anomalies. Although these systems are legal, the problem is that the technology that's being developed is at the expense of those on the other side of the transaction – namely, the retail customer."

"How about you, Ms. Baxter?"

"Well I'm thinking of doing my thesis on risk and return, specifically how investors evaluate risk and measure return. At present, I haven't decided on the scope of my studies or the specific topics that I'll cover and how much original research that will be required."

Carlos whispered to Ike, "See, I told you. All work and no play."

Harry now realized that when Snookie spoke, her words were effortlessly chosen and arranged in an order so that the tone and atmosphere created some effect she wanted to have on this group of young men who were now at the height of their sexual hormone activity.

It'll be a while before they'll learn of her awesome intellectual power, the range of her skills, her dedication to each task and her vicious competitive spirit.

"Mr. Thompson, would you please share with the class your reason for being here?"

Larry Thompson was the son of a successful steel company executive.

"For my PhD thesis, I'll be focusing on a portion of the field of Economics and a compilation of facts for investors that I intend compile and publish annually. It will tell the investor how to use the data as well."

"Let me know if you need some help," Snookie said, matter-of-factly. Larry smiled, nervously.

"Alright," said Harry. "Now that we know each other, I want you to know that you've all been personally selected for this special workshop by me, because you each have a particular special talent that we are going to need to accomplish our goal."

"What's the goal?" asked Carlos.

"I'm glad you asked," said Harry. You – all of you – and I – we're going to save the world."

CHAPTER SEVEN THE LONGEST RIDE

Carlos picked up his iPhone, but he had no signal. It looked like his Wifi was still working, so he sent a "WhatsApp" text to Bob.

Dude, are you safe?

Carlos could see that the message had been received right away. Bob texted back: Barely. Almost got caught in a bank war.

You still downtown?

Yes.

Meet me outside your office in an hour. We've got to get to the airport.

Carlos finished packing. He packed as if he didn't know whether or not he would ever come back to his apartment. His carry-on bag contained his laptop, a stash of dollars and euros, gold coins, his passport, and a folder with important papers. Once the packing was done, he sat on the couch to think and make sure he hadn't forgotten anything. He looked around as if to say good-bye to the apartment, then, satisfied nothing was forgotten, he called the driver, who indicated that he was downstairs in the parking garage waiting. Carlos pulled up the handles on his suitcase and carry-on and took a last look around.

"I'll be back. I hope."

He turned, opened the door, and walked out, rolling the bags behind him.

Down in the parking garage, Henry, the driver, exited the black Lincoln and greeted Carlos, with a warm smile and hand shake. He put his luggage in the trunk of the car.

"Looks like you're leaving for a vacation. I thought it was just a short trip."

"Under these circumstances, you never know."

The car pulled out of the parking lot and it was a slow crawl to the I90. Once they got on the onramp, it seemed even slower.

"I think we should get off and take South Clark Street. Might be better."

"You're the pro, man."

As they crept down Clark Street, they saw nothing but chaos. The local Target store had been besieged by a large mob of looters, some of whom were running down the street pushing shopping carts full of food and merchandise. News crews were running about, catching everything on video. The police seemed to be just letting the looters go. They were more concerned with protecting the firemen, who were responding to a blazing fire in the parking garage.

"Look at that. The police aren't doing nuthin."

"They're too busy arresting protesters at the Federal Reserve to worry about Target."

"It's a damn shame."

"It sure is, Henry. And it's going to get worse. This is just the beginning."

***

Bob waited outside his office building, his bags packed, nervously puffing on a cigarette. A beggar came by, holding out his hand.

"Got some spare change for a guy hard on his luck?"

"Dude, everyone's hard on their luck. You probably have more change in your pocket than me! Here, have a cigarette."

Bob held out a cigarette, and the man grumbled, took it, and walked away without so much as a thank you.

Carlos and Henry pulled up and Carlos rolled down the rear window and waved to Bob.

"Man, I didn't know you smoke!"

"I quit about two years ago. Just took it back up today."

"Well, toss it out. Henry doesn't allow smoking in his car."

Bob threw his cigarette down, crushed it under his foot, put his bags in the trunk and slid in the back seat next to Carlos.

"Ready for the longest 15 minute ride of your life?"

They drove through the smoking streets, dodging fire trucks and police cars. Outside a Walgreen's store, a group of cops was confronting a band of looters who had just exited with their spoils. As the thieves crunched through the glass snow on the sidewalk that used to be the shop windows, the police alerted them to stop.

They ran in all directions, and the cops pursued on foot. Another band of looters, seeing the police car left unattended, got together and started pushing the squad car. More and more rioters joined them, rocking the car back and forth, until they finally pushed it completely over. Then, they lit it on fire. Henry rolled by the bizarre seen while they all gaped in awe.

"Teamwork."

"Yeah, Bob. That's the power of the people. Too bad they didn't use it the way they should have before it was too late."

CHAPTER EIGHT APOCALYPSE? NOW?

The students looked up at Harry with surprise, as if they could not believe what they had heard.

"I'll bet you didn't think a handful of economists could save the world, did you? You thought our world as we know it would end with nuclear war or something like that? No, it's much more basic than that. It's more likely going to be from a disruption in the water supply, power and lack of food as a result of an economic collapse. Either that or a financial war."

"Financial war?"

"Yes. Our automated trading and banking systems are just as susceptible to cyberattack as our buildings are to a physical terrorist attack."

Harry paused a while for his whiz kids to get a handle on the problem.

"That's why your participation in this class is important, not only for your own purposes, but the benevolent task that I have indentured you all for."

"What is the task?" asked Snookie.

"We're going to help the Congress to help the people by giving them the tools they need to save the world economy from collapse."

Harry regarded the students seriously, so that they could see that this was no joke.

"What makes you so sure that we're on the verge of a collapse?" asked Carlos.

"Well now, I don't have to tell you that I've been around a little longer than you."

Harry smiled, and the group collectively chuckled.

"I had a front row seat in 1998 when Wall Street bailed out the failing hedge funds. We missed the bullet back then, but we never learned because ten years later, as a result of the burst of the housing bubble, the big banks were on the verge of failure, but we just printed more dollars and bailed them out.

"We won't be able to print ourselves out of the next crisis, I'm afraid."

"Why not?" asked Ike.

"Can anyone answer Mr. Pendelton's question?"

Snookie stood up. "Because the U.S. Dollar is a liability on the Fed's balance sheet. It's only money if we believe it's money."

"That's right, Ms. Baxter. You're almost there. And why is it only money if we believe it's money?"

"Because everything is digital. The banks control your money. The dollar is actually nothing more than a liability – a promise to pay."

"It's a fiat currency," said Harry. "Does anyone know what that means? Yes, Mr. Rodriguez?"

"We know it only too well in Mexico. A fiat currency is one that the state orders that a particular form of money serves as legal currency."

"That is correct. It's money because the state says it's money."

"It's a contract, isn't it?"

"Yes, Mr. Thompson. And, for our fiat dollar, who are the parties to that contract?"

"The Federal Reserve, who issues the money, and the U.S. Treasury, who provides the collateral for the notes by issuing treasury securities."

"That's right, Mr. Thompson. They've been printing about $80 billion per month to avoid a collapse of the U.S. financial system.

"But, professor, you're talking about the dollar as a world reserve currency. If the dollar loses its value, then the U.S. Treasury won't be able to pay its debts, isn't that right?"

"Yes, and, in fact, any catastrophic event, such as the near bank failures of 2008, could cause the collapse of the dollar, which would also collapse the euro, because the dollar is its reserve currency. And, once the world stops using the dollar as its reserve currency, all the functioning economies in the western world will collapse.

"What that means is that prices for everything will go up 300-400%, as foreign exporters reject the dollar for trade. Since those exports can only be bought in another currency, it will take massive amounts of dollars to buy that currency. People who had enough money to live on before will realize that their money's buying power has been eliminated, and they won't be able to buy food. The food supply itself, which operates on very small profit margins and survives only as a result of prompt payment of invoices, will come to a screeching halt because the huge chains like Walmart will fail."

"What about the Government? Can't they stop a crisis like you're talking about?"

"That's a legitimate question, Mr. Rodriguez. The Federal Reserve will try to make the dollar attractive to foreign investors, by raising interest rates. But this will only lead to the destabilization of the stock markets and the failure of the "too big to fail banks" who've relied on no-interest loans from the Fed to gamble on risky investments to earn a profit. All this, in turn, will lead to the biggest real estate market crash in history, as the deflation the Fed has been staving off eliminates the value of almost all assets, which will be followed by a tidal wave of inflation.

"As people struggle to purchase the necessities of life, which will become more and more scarce, this will drive prices even higher. The Government will be unable to collect enough dollars to keep rolling over its massive debt, and will simply be unable to pay for anything. That's why printing more money won't get us out of the next crisis."

"So what do we do?" asked Bob. "Bend over and kiss our butts good-bye?"

Harry smiled as the entire class erupted in laughter, except for Snookie.

"Of course not. We have to act now while we still have a functioning economy to save. We've known for over fifty years that the financial industry has been methodically cheating the public by charging them for services that are worthless as demonstrated by countless peer reviewed studies by academia and their students. And we've known for at least 12 years that the banks are trading in almost unregulated and risky derivatives, with notional values larger than the world economy.

"I believe that the banks and the financial services industry take more than their share of our profits by using unfair business tactics. It now appears that our entire financial system has taken far more risk that is warranted by its capital structure and that this will lead to a market crash affecting economies world-wide. As for 'what do we do,' that part is up to you."

"Us?" asked Carlos.

"Yes," said Harry. "And there's no time to lose."

CHAPTER NINE SHAKEN

Ike charged at the two men. The second one ran, but the first held his ground, let go of the slim-jim and flipped out a knife. Ike stopped short of his reach.

"Gimme the keys or I'll kill you." He hissed like a snake, through a set of mangled teeth, as he shook the knife at Ike.

"Try it!"

The man lunged at Ike with the blade and Snookie screamed. Ike moved to the right, out of his way, hopping lightly on his feet.

"Dancing won't help you," said the man, as he ran at Ike, swinging the knife in front of him wildly back and forth. Ike threw back his hips at the man's forward thrust, grabbed his knife-wielding wrist with his left hand and struck his wrist hard with the right, and the knife clacked to the ground. The man turned and ran away. Snookie ran to Ike and embraced him, then suddenly backed off.

"Ike, are you okay?"

"I'm fine, just a little shaken. Let's get out of here!"

Ike opened the door and ushered Snookie into the car, throwing the suitcases in the trunk.

"Do you have cash?" Ike asked, as he accelerated out of the parking lot. "Anything we can trade for gas?"

"I've got some, and some gold as well, in case nobody wants to take cash."

"Good. But I'm afraid the guy with the knife is not the only desperate person we're going to run across."

"Let's hope the next one is less deadly."

Ike navigated their way out of O'Hare, wasting precious gas in the stop and go traffic, until finally they were on the road. They crept along what should have been a relatively quick route, even in rush hour, until they reached the I80, which was still open but creeping along, stop and go at about 5 miles per hour.

"It's like the world's gone crazy, Ike."

"Yeah. Harry was right."

CHAPTER TEN HOW IT ALL WORKS

Harry wrote a single phrase on the blackboard: The Stock Market. Once everyone had come to order, he spoke.

"Does anyone know how the stock market works?"

Snookie raised her hand.

"Ms. Baxter, tell us what you think."

"Thank you, professor. I'll try. It's basically like any other kind of market, where people buy and sell. Trading of marketable securities started on 1791 under a buttonwood tree in lower Manhattan Island. Picture it late in the afternoon, when the garbage wagons, pulled by horses, passed by on their way to barges that will haul off the refuse to a dump site offshore. A huge herd of wild pigs would follow the wagons, forcing the brokers to pack up their card tables where they had laid out all the stock certificates they had for sale. When trading was slow, the brokers gathered up the stone rubble in the vicinity and build a wall around the tree, and that's how Wall Street got its name."

She's like an encyclopedia. Dates, numbers, everything!

"Very good, Ms. Baxter. Perhaps we should have you teach the class."

Everyone snickered at that thought, except of course, for Snookie, and Carlos and Ike, who both thought it was a fine idea. Harry continued.

"The following year, all the larger traders formed the New York Stock Exchange and signed what was called the "Buttonwood Agreement." Those brokers who had been left out formed their own organization called the "CURB" and literally stood out on the sidewalk for the next one hundred and thirty years, trading their securities using hand signals with other brokers hanging out the windows of the offices on the street. It wasn't until 1921 that CURB changed its name to the American Stock Exchange and moved into their own building out of the rain and snow. The CURB today is known as the American Stock Exchange, or AMEX.

"Does anyone know what makes the NASDAQ exchange different from the New York or American Exchanges?"

Snookie raised her hand again. "Ms. Baxter?"

"The NASDAQ Exchange meets in cyber space and consists of a network of 50,000 computers where trading is done electronically. These trades are executed in under one second. In fact, some large firms have sophisticated trading systems that use programs to gain a few microseconds advantages over other slower and less sophisticated systems."

"Very good, Ms. Baxter. Is there anything you don't know?"

That comment sent another round of laughter through the lecture hall, but Snookie didn't even crack a smile. Harry scratched his head.

She's so serious all the time. Just like a computer.

"At 9:30 AM Eastern Standard time, trading starts on the NYSE Monday through Friday, except for holidays. The markets to the east in Europe have been open and trading for three hours now while the markets in the orient have been closed for some time.

"By the end of the day our domestic markets are open twenty-four hours a day, Monday through Friday. And, by the end of our domestic markets' trading day, some five billion shares will have changed hands.

"Approximately 80% to 90% of the shares that exchange hands are traded by professional portfolio managers acting for large mutual funds, pension funds and trusts, and by speculators with trading rights who keep the market functioning with arbitrage activities throughout the day. The rest of the trading activity is represented by individual shareholders whose buy and sell orders are executed by their retail brokers.

"Does anyone know how market prices move?"

Bob Brammon raised his hand. "Mr. Brammon?"

"Market prices move on the basis of random events that become known throughout the day and that some of the events may have been anticipated by the market while other events were not anticipated by the market and appear at random. It is not at all unusual for the price to fall on a security when a dividend is raised when a higher dividend was anticipated by the market."

"That's correct, Mr. Brammon. After all, investors are human and it seems that their emotions drive swings in the market. That's something Mr. Pendleton may care to elaborate on later. Market prices change on fresh news. But, what you may have read in the financial press, or in a broker's analyst report is already old news by the time you've seen it, and has already been digested by the market and incorporated into prices for the security."

"I might add, class, that Mr. Brammon's work here at the University is sponsored by his employer, a major Wall Street investment banker. He's here doing original research using quantitative techniques and I'm certain that he will be of great value to the group in evaluating the role that risk took in the melt-down our financial system in 2008.

"Remember, our class project is to concentrate on the damage and impact that the financial industry has done to millions of shareholders and to recommend changes in the financial system to prevent a repeat, if at all possible. I hope that we can come up with some reasonable recommendations for our government to pursue without damaging our country's ability to allocate capital among the companies here in America. We have the best and most robust method of distributing venture capital that has ever been invented, and I would hate to see all that go down the drain.

Ike raised his hand. "Professor, I think the study of neuroe-conomics can be very useful to solving our crisis."

Harry smiled. "Well, Mr. Pendleton, please tell us how."

Ike turned to Snookie and smiled proudly. She didn't even flinch a reaction.

"Uh, yes, sir. I believe there are two problems facing the average 'man on the street' investor. First is his lack of information on how to invest in marketable securities, including his almost religious faith in what his broker tells him. Secondly, it's those things that go on in his mind when he's faced with the decisions that must be made during the investment process.

"In my opinion, I believe the worse enemy of the investor is that fellow he sees in his mirror as he shaves every day. Neuroe-conomics is a relatively new field of economics, where economists are studying how the mind, specifically the limbic system, works to mislead us when we are confronted with sensory signals that take over our minds when making financial decisions."

"Very pertinent indeed, Mr. Pendleton. I look forward to your contribution, and I'd like to see how it comports with Mr. Brammon's findings. Now class, we've run out of time, but saving the world will not wait, so I will be available at my office on campus anytime you need me. Please be prepared to discuss when we meet again what type of contribution each one of your disciplines can make."

Snookie waited until the room cleared and then approached Harry while he was packing up. Harry was looking all around the table, and seemed frustrated.

"Professor Mason?"

"Yes, Ms. Baxter?" Harry looked up at her, then back at the table.

"Are you looking for something?"

"I seem to have lost my glasses."

"Professor, you're wearing them."

Harry felt his glasses, just to make sure they were really there, and smiled.

"Oh, my goodness. You're right!"

Harry continued to pack up his briefcase, then paused.

"I'm sorry, Ms. Baxter, did you have a question?"

"Yes, professor. Are you really serious about saving the world, or is it just a learning exercise for the class?"

"My dear, everything in life is a learning exercise. But, serious? Yes, I'm dead serious. I think that, unless we do something and do it quickly, we may be going back to an economic stone age."

CHAPTER ELEVEN ARMAGEDDON

Carlos and Henry stopped on their trip to Midway to pick up Harry and his wife, Jennifer.

Harry opened the door for Jennifer, then slid in next to her.

Carlos looked at Harry in shock, when he saw the Band-Aid on Harry's face and the scrapes on his hand.

"What happened to you, professor?"

"Nothing, just a few scrapes. Anybody able to get any news on the radio?"

"It comes and goes."

"Use the dial, not the digital shortcut. I remember when all radios had just dials."

Carlos fiddled with the radio dial, and an AM station crackled to life.

Members of the House Committee on Terrorism have proposed wide-sweeping reform to the visa waiver program, with House Speak Nettle Winehard proposing an outright ban on Muslims.

"How ignorant. It's not the Muslims who caused this problem. They should call for a ban on the industrial military complex."

Now we will go live to the White House, where the president is addressing the nation.

"My fellow Americans, in this time of crisis, we must all stick together. Panic is not going to help, and just feeds the enemy. I've put together a task force from the FBI and the Department of Home Security and they're working diligently to keep the American public safe. The FDIC and the Federal Reserve are both doing their jobs, and I can assure you that these measures will stabilize our economy.

"They always approach everything as if it were a war. The terrorist attacks created very small casualties themselves, but the panic triggered an economic collapse of gigantic proportions."

"And, I remember what you said, professor. Printing money is not going to get us out of this."

"No, Mr. Rodriguez, it's not. But neither is putting an army on the streets. The elite are scrambling to do something to protect themselves."

"Not us."

"Of course not us, Mr. Brammon. Our only use to them is to be a consumer at the bottom of the food chain."

"What about the FDIC?"

"What about it?"

"Won't they pay off depositors like they did with the savings and loan failures?"

"They can't, Mr. Brammon. Bank of America failed because of its derivative gambles. It doesn't have any more money. The derivatives get paid off first. There's only about $46 billion in the FDIC fund and over $4.5 trillion in deposits."

"So the big banks have had it?"

\"No, Mr. Rodriguez, the little banks have had it. They'll all go bankrupt and there will only be five banks left. They truly are too big to fail."

When they got to the airport, they found Larry waiting outside the private terminal. He had made it just in time. They exited the car.

"Good luck, Henry."

"You too, Carlos. Give them hell on the hill!" Henry shook his fist and drove off as Carlos waved.

Harry was happy to see Larry Thompson. He smiled and shook his hand.

"Glad you could make it, Mr. Thompson. Have you heard from Mr. Pendleton and Ms. Baxter?"

"No, professor. Last I heard they were both flying out of O'Hare."

Harry frowned. "I hope they made it. We need them in Washington."

"If there still is a Washington."

"O'Hare is closed. That's why I asked. We've been trying to call them, with no luck."

When they got inside the terminal, they learned that the pilot and co-pilot were already on the plane. The co-pilot came out to the gate to hurry them on.

"If we're going to get out of here at all, we have to try to do it now."

"We have two more people who may need a ride."

The co-pilot just pointed to his watch. "Five minutes."

He rushed back onto the plane.

After five minutes of calling and waiting, they all boarded the jet.

"We're just going to have to pray they make it."

The pilots went through their routine checks and were ready to take off.

"We've been cleared for takeoff."

Then, they received another call from air traffic control.

"Sorry, folks. There's going to be a slight delay."

"What's the holdup?"

The pilot looked back in frustration.

"They say they can clear us for takeoff, but we'll be the last ones and they can't guarantee we'll be able to land at Ronald Reagan."

"Why not?"

"Air traffic controller's strike. A lot of airports are closed. O'Hare's been having rolling blackouts affecting air traffic control, so they've closed it and cancelled all flights."

Carlos thought of his friends who had declined his offer to fly them in his father's jet.

"We've got clearance. We're number ten for takeoff."

The plane taxied into a line of small aircraft. Everyone wanted to get to someplace better, wherever that was.

CHAPTER TWELVE HOME AWAY FROM HOME

Harry's study was furnished and equipped with several computer workstations and a high definition TV screen hooked up to those stations. In this manner, the workstations could access the main frame on campus and then, via dedicated fiber optic cables, the large-scale high-speed computers located at the University of California, and MIT. Only the Pentagon could rival the computing power at his disposal. At all times throughout each day, you could find several of his graduate students there, working on their individual projects. With Harry nearby, they could ask a question or two without interrupting his work and without waiting for the next class.

In one corner of the room, an African gray parrot, named "Jackpot," was watching CNBC on the monitor, commenting on the market as he watched the red and green arrows, indicating an up market when green and a down market when red, flash across the screen.

"Market is up today! Cramer says sell!"

Harry's wife, Jennifer, a financial expert in her own right, and about 20 years his junior, had her own desk in the study, which she used as her office as well. She was a lovely woman, with porcelain skin, and strawberry blonde hair. More impressive than her beauty was her grace in movement. There was a knock at the door, which Jackpot mimicked perfectly. As Jennifer walked to the door to answer it, she drifted across the floor with the finesse of a figure skater. "Harry, it's June Lockheed from the Financial Digest – your 11:00 appointment."

"Pork bellies are up! Cramer says sell! Sell!"

Who is this June? Do I know her? Since his mini-stroke last summer, Harry was having trouble remembering appointments, faces, and people's names. Jennifer showed June into the study.

"June, this my husband, Harry. I'll leave you two alone for now."

"Have a seat, June." Harry motioned to one of the soft chairs in front of his desk and June took a seat. Harry sat in a chair next to her. She was a pretty young woman, dressed demurely in a grey business suit, and Harry could see that she was hiding a pair of beautiful turquoise eyes behind her conservative looking glasses, perhaps in an attempt to disguise her beauty, and to appear more serious in business.

"Market is up! Market is up! Cramer says sell!"

Jackpot danced on his perch, moving his head back and forth in a circular motion.

"You watch Cramer?"

"More for entertainment than anything else, but Jackpot here thinks he's cool."

June smiled. "Hello, Jackpot."

"Hello, Jackpot. Cramer says sell. Hello, Jackpot, hello."

"So, what is the Financial Digest and how come I've never heard of it?"

"It's brand new. I founded the digest only a few months ago. I distribute it by Email and only accept advertisers who are Certified Financial Planners or Registered Investment Advisors."

"It sounds interesting, but what's it got to do with me?"

"I just thought perhaps you may want to make some comments on our current financial crisis. It's interesting to hear everyone say that we're in a recovery and you say that we're in a depression."

"That's not an original idea, June. John Meynard Keynes defined a depression as a prolonged period of below-trend growth, which neither collapses nor goes back to trend. The Government's just afraid to call it what it is because they don't want to cause a panic."

"Can I quote you on that?"

"If you like. Say, I've got a bunch of students working on a solution to the current economic crisis. You may want to talk to them, as soon as they're ready with their findings."

"I would love to, thanks."

"Now I have a question for you, June. Have you gathered any stories of people who have been really hurt by the financial meltdown?

"Yes, yes, I have. I've had a couple of clients who were really hurt. I'm a registered investment advisor and they came to me for consulting."

"Cramer says sell!"

"Tell me about them."

"It was a cowboy-type and his wife. They were potential clients who had been taken by their broker. Since, I'm a Registered Investment Advisor, I have a fiduciary duty to my clients to provide them with a stock portfolio that meets their needs and ability to take risk as compared to a stock broker who is just a salesman, and mostly acts in his own interests. Like Woody Allen said, "Your broker invests your money until it is all gone.""

"Brokers!" Harry puffed out the word in frustration.

"Brokers are thieves!"

June looked at Jackpot, then back at Harry and smiled. "Can I quote Jackpot on that one?"

"If you like."

"Anyway, the client's name was Tex. He and his wife came to my office with such trepidation that I thought he may get up and leave at any time. She looked as if she wanted to get the meeting over as soon as possible.

The look on Tex's face was that of complete defeat, and Glenda, his wife, sat in her chair as if she was sitting on top of a dozen eggs.

"We brought our historical account statements like you asked, June."

Tex tossed the papers on the conference table as if, by this action, all their problems would disappear, and Glenda started to cry while June looked through the papers.

"I see that your broker's opened a margin account for you."

June flipped through the statements.

"Looks like he churned the securities in the account weekly, which made a lot of profits for himself and his company when the market was going up, but when the market collapsed, the margin calls wiped you out."

"Damn right they did!"

"Looks like the market value of your portfolio barely covered what you owed."

"Isn't there anything I can do?" Tex looked like a lost little boy.

"When you opened the margin account, you gave your broker the authority to trade your account as he saw fit, and you also agreed to arbitration by an arbitrator appointed by the industry."

"So there's no way I can sue this mother-"

"Dear..."

"...This guy for wasting all our money?"

"Not in my opinion. But I'm not a lawyer."

"We've already been to lawyers. They say the same thing as you."

"I'd been hearing stories like this for several years and it was always the same. Tex's broker, Steve, had been with the firm for twenty five years. He was a high school dropout and, for several years he did day labor jobs and some landscaping while he worked on his GED. Then, his father suggested that he join his country club as an associate member. Herbert Benchman, the manager of a local brokerage firm asked Steve if he knew a lot of the members of the country club, and he said yes. It wasn't long until Steve has passed his series 7 exam and was part of the firm, converting country club members to clients."

"He found his calling."

"Apparently, but he knew nothing about investing. He put his new clients into options and futures, and became one of the company's most successful brokers. Clients lost all their money, though."

"Of course."

"But that's not the end of the story."

"Go on."

"As he was leaving my office, after I told him he probably had no recourse other than arbitration, Tex said, "We'll see about that." About a week later, the headlines read, 'Broker Branded'. Tex had invited Steve to a barbecue at his house and ended up branding him with an "X" right on his rear end."

Harry laughed. "I'm sorry. I don't condone that type of behavior, but it's kind of funny. And deserving."

Jackpot squawked and laughed with Harry.

"I see Jackpot agrees. I think that Steve was lucky that Tex didn't kill him. But, of course, Tex is the one they put in jail."

"Of course."

"The story sent ripples through the industry, not because of the violence, but what Tex's case revealed about their practices and procedures."

"June, I'd like you to consider talking to my group of graduate students while they try to figure out a solution to these types of problems. They could benefit by your stories."

"I'd be honored."

***

Harry had fallen asleep at his computer. Jennifer put her hand on his head and stroked the thinning grey hair, and this startled him to wake.

"Where am I?"

"At the office. Time to go home, Harry. Even Nobel laureates need their rest."

Time to go home!

Harry stretched and yawned, then stood up and felt his pockets.

"Have you seen my keys?"

"Check on your desk."

Harry looked around the desk, and, sure enough, he found them there, just like she said.

"Let's go, Harry. Tomorrow will come around sooner than you think."

"Yes, yes. Let's go."

"Let's go! Let's go!"

Jennifer opened Jackpot's travel cage and he hopped from his perch into the cage. Harry smiled and followed her to the door. He put his jacket on, then paused, patting at his jacket pockets.

"Hon?"

"Hmm?"

"Have you seen my keys?"

"Harry, you just asked me that. They were on your desk and now they're probably in your pants pocket."

He felt his pocket.

There they are!

Harry chuckled. "You're right, I had them all along."

"It's probably stress, putting a strain on you. Maybe you can ask Dr. Reynolds for something to, you know, take the edge off."

"I don't know if I want to take anything, Jennifer. Don't I have an appointment with him to go over the results of my physical?"

"Yes."

"When?"

"It's next Wednesday, Harry. I reminded you yesterday."

"Guess I just wasn't paying attention."

CHAPTER THIRTEEN ON THE RUN

It was slow going on the I80 as hundreds of cars jammed together to make the exodus from Chicago. Ike looked in the rear view mirror at the city, which was hard to see through all the smoke from the fires.

"It used to remind me of the Emerald City in the Wizard of Oz. You'd drive through miles and miles of cornfields, and, all of a sudden, there it would be, rising the in distance, and shining, just like a jewel. Now, I can hardly see it."

"Yes. This must have been how they felt in 1871 during the Great Chicago Fire."

Ike looked at Snookie. It was strange that she had said that so devoid of emotion. He shook it off.

"Where did you learn to fight like that?"

"I was an MMA addict in high school. Hung out in the gym whenever I wasn't studying. They teach you how to disarm an attacker. Never thought I'd have to use it."

"I never thought anything like this would ever happen."

"Me neither, but if the pattern is correct, we should be thinking about where to get food and gas, and try to get as much of it as we can before our money becomes worthless. You stay here. I'm going to go find out what I can."

Ike left the car among the others in the traffic jam and approached a group of men that had gathered outside their vehicles. Some of them were smoking, nervously.

"Hey, guys, you know where we can get something to eat and gas up?"

One of the men flicked his cigarette butt and said, "You can forget about gassing up, at least around here. I've tried. But, there's a guy down the road there selling stuff. You may want to check it out."

"Much obliged."

Ike went back to tell Snookie that he was scouting for food, and she replaced him in the driver's seat in case traffic started to move again.

"Be careful, Ike."

Ike struck a Ninja pose, winked, and then was off.

"Snookie tried her phone again. No signal. She fired up the car radio. There was nothing on the FM channels except static. The AM channels showed more promise as she surfed through them.

"The president has declared the existence of an unusual and extraordinary threat to the national security and economy of the United States, and has invoked the powers of the International Emergency Economic Powers Act, blocking assets of groups the FBI suspects were involved in the hacking of critical transportation, energy and food distribution systems."

"Congress, in a special session, has authorized the United States military reserves to be activated to help local authorities respond to the rioting that has overcome every major U.S. city. Local authorities are warning everyone to stay inside. Rolling blackouts have been reported in major metropolitan areas throughout the country."

Ike approached a huge crowd that had formed around what looked like a truck with a mobile farm stand that had parked on the shoulder of the road.

This must be it. What's so special about a farm stand?

The people in the crowd were pushing, each one trying to get to the front of the line first. Ike stepped up on his toes to look over them. It's just a guy selling fruit and vegetables. He shouted out to him.

"You got any water? Anything to drink?"

"Yeah, I've got some well water here. A hundred bucks for a five gallon drum."

The crowd reacted with a collective groan.

"A hundred bucks!"

"Take it or leave it."

"I'll take one," piped up Ike, holding out a one hundred dollar bill, and barging through the line.

"Please let the customer through, folks." The man took the bill and gave Ike the water bottle.

"Anything else, young man?"

"Yes."

Ike picked out as much fruit and vegetables as he could hold, along with the water. The man weighed and tallied them on his calculator.

"That'll be five hundred, including the water."

Ike handed over another four hundred dollar bills. The ice being broken, more people in the crowd started asking for water and waving hundred dollar bills.

Neuroeconomics in action.

CHAPTER FOURTEEN IKE AND NOAH

In his lab, Ike looked more like a zookeeper than an economist. There were cages of rats and rabbits, birds and two monkeys, one of which Ike had let loose and was sitting next to him in the lab.

"We have at least two of everyone, Chester. I feel just like Noah with his ark." Ike laughed.

Chester jumped up and down, reacting to Ike's laughter, which made Ike laugh even harder.

"Chester, we're having visitors today, so be on your best behavior, okay?" Ike nodded to Chester and he nodded back.

When Carlos walked in and saw Chester, he we jumped a step back, his arms outstretched. Chester jumped up and down and squealed.

"Whoa!"

"Don't worry, Carlos. He's friendly. Smart too. Sit down, I'll show you."

"Next to him?"

Carlos motioned with his thumb and made a face.

"Yeah. Right on the couch."

Carlos tentatively sat down on left side of the couch, trying to sit as far away from Chester as possible.

"Don't be scared, Carlos. He won't hurt you."

"Dude, I'm not scared."

"Chester, this is Carlos. He's happy to meet you."

Chester stuck out his hand.

"Well?"

"Well, what?"

"Aren't you going to shake his hand?"

Carlos put out his hand, and Chester took it with both of his and shook it up and down, making Carlos smile.

"That's cool."

"Who else is coming?"

"Bob and Larry, I think."

"What about Snookie?"

"She says she doesn't understand what animals have to do with economics."

"Right. Maybe if she showed up, she would understand. Would you like some tea while you wait?"

"Sure, thanks."

"Thank Chester. Chester, would you please get Carlos a can of tea?"

Chester jumped off the couch, went to the small refrigerator, opened it and took out a can of tea. He hopped over back to Carlos and presented it to him.

"Thanks, Chester."

Ike gave Chester a treat for a reward. "Very well done, Chester."

There was a knock on the door.

"Come in."

Bob and Larry entered the lab, both pointing at the monkey, who pointed back at them, comically.

"Hey guys, meet Chester. Chester, this is Bob, and this is Larry."

Chester shook Larry's hand, then Bob's hand, and Ike gave him a treat.

"Thanks for coming to the lab, guys. Here we study which areas of the brain are responsible for which types of decision processes."

"So, you're really a scientist as well as an economist, right?"

"I guess so, yeah. You can't really study an investor's decision making process without considering the brain. Chester here is going to show us an experiment with his partner, the lovely Lolita. Chester, bring Lolita out, would you please?"

Chester opened the door of Lolita's cage and she came out and stood before them. Unlike Chester, who was in his birthday suit, she was dressed in a red skirt with white polka dots for the students' visit.

Ike fitted Chester and Lolita with a special electrode equipped helmet, hooked them up to the instrument panel, and gave them each a reward.

"Neuroeconomics studies the parts of the brain that help us to make decisions. To study risk, we're going to examine the firing rates of the neurons in the orbitofrontal cortex of these monkeys. This was an experiment originated by Padoa-Schioppa & Assad in 2006.

"Frank Knight, an economist, defined risk in the 1920's as a quantity with known outcome values and known outcome probabilities, and ambiguity as a quantity with known outcomes and unknown probabilities. He said that risk was a measurable quantity of uncertainty that is distinct from ambiguity, which is an unmeasurable uncertainty.

"We've inserted electrodes in both Chester and Lolita's orbitofrontal cortex, which is the part of the brain associated with decision making. That's this part of the brain." Ike pointed to a diagram of the brain on the wall, where a highlighted portion of the frontal lobe was located just behind the eyes."

Ike positioned Chester and Lolita on a chair in front of two separate computer screens.

"Watch the monkeys make their choices buy pointing to choices on what risks to take. The higher the risk, the more juice they get."

"How do they make their choices?"

"There are two kinds of juice. Each juice is represented by the colored squares that appear on the monitor. The more colored squares, the greater amount of juice they get. They make their choices with eye movements, and the computer disperses the juice they choose through these tubes."

"Then, why don't they just pick the highest number of squares each time?"

"Because, sometimes, when they do, the computer doesn't deliver any juice. Picking the lower amount gets them juice every time, but in a smaller amount."

They watched as Ike and the monkeys performed the experiment.

"See, they're taking a risk whether or not the juice will be delivered."

"They're choosing to get the most juice, no matter whether the risk is higher or not."

"That's right, Carlos."

"They're greedy."

"No, Bob, they're taking a risk to get the highest return."

Ike showed them a graph printout from the experiment.

"This is a printout of a longer experimental period. They have consistently taken a greater risk to receive a bigger reward."

Bob stared at the graphs. "Fascinating."

"With humans, our studies show that we would rather not lose a certain amount of money more than we relish earning the same amount of money. We also learn that, over time, our decision making changes. People who choose one candy bar today over two tomorrow are making an impulsive choice. But, give them the same decision over 1 candy bar in 100 days or 2 candy bars in 101 days, and they opt for two."

"Interesting. So, all this monkey business explains how brokers cheat their clients by offering them investments with higher returns and greater risks."

"Watch it Larry, we don't all cheat clients," said Bob.

CHAPTER FIFTEEN THE LONG AND WINDING ROAD

Ike got back to the car just as things started moving on the interstate. Snookie popped the trunk and Ike threw the water in the back and jumped into the passenger's seat with the bags of fruit, as the motorists behind him started to honk their horns in protest.

"I was getting worried."

"Thanks, Snook. It's good to know that someone cares."

"It's very scary. The phones still don't work, so I can't call my parents. The radio works, but it's all bad news – they're talking about the military being authorized to help quell social disturbances in all major cities."

"Sounds like martial law."

"Isn't that unconstitutional?"

"Yup. It's a complete suspension of the Constitution. But there is precedent for it. Lincoln was the first president to use it during the Civil War. You heard anything about the bank runs?"

"They're being silent on that."

"That's no surprise. I heard some of the people out there saying that they went to their banks to get out their money and they refused to give it to them."

"That's because it's not their money."

"You sound just like Harry."

"Once you deposit that money in your checking account, it becomes the bank's money and you're just another one of their creditors. That's why they have been going all digital with money – credit cards, debit cards, wiring money – it's all digital. There are no shipments of cash to cover all those transactions."

"And that's why Harry told us to have at least a six month supply of cash on hand."

"And to use about 10% of your investing money to buy gold."

"I'm beginning to see that his course was really worth the tuition."

"Where should I go, Ike?"

"Just keep going as long as traffic is flowing. When reach the countryside, we can get off and look for gas."

"It's only a twelve hour drive."

"It could be longer than that. And once we run out of gas, it's game over."

Snookie and Ike crawled along the interstate, watching plumes of smoke in the distance as Chicago burned.

***

Carlos's plane finally took off, and Harry looked down at the burning city with sadness. He squeezed Jennifer's hand.

"Look at that. I always loved that place. I thought it would have been climate change, not citizens burning their own city down."

"Climate change?"

"Yeah. They didn't have a plan for that any more than they did for the economy. Just a lot of talk."

"And the economy did us in first."

"Let's not give up hope, Mr. Rodriguez."

CHAPTER SIXTEEN THE PROFIT IN POLITICS

Harry wrote three words on the board in succession: 1. Problem 2. Cause 3. Solution.

"We will be joined by some experts tomorrow to tell us about what they have learned about the damage that has already been done to the average investor, insurance firms and pension funds."

Harry paused for a moment at the board, staring ahead as though he were in deep thought.

"Professor?"

"Yes, Mr. Brammon?"

Harry realized that he had been staring into space.

"Oh, excuse me, um, before we bring the experts in, I want to hear why you think we got into this mess, who's to blame and how another event can be avoided. Mr. Brammon, let's hear from you first."

"Well professor, I think that Wall Street is responsible for the problem and that it can be solved with additional rules and regulations."

"What about you, Mr. Rodriguez? Do you think we can blame the whole thing on Wall Street?"

"Well, I think the problem is much deeper than you suggest. For years your country has been, little by little, destroying those elements of your economic system that had made it successful. In a free market system, funds flow to places where the highest returns are available. This automatic system assures that goods and services are provided at the highest quality at the lowest prices. When you start tinkering with how resources are used you run the risk that you introduce inefficiencies."

"So, you agree with Mr. Brammon that the Government is to blame, not because it didn't regulate enough, but because it regulated too much."

"The Government and the central banks that control the money supply are to blame. In a capitalistic system, returns on investments are allocated according to the risks involved and the higher the risk, the higher the monetary reward. In my country – Mexico – our economic system does not work this way and so our people are not so fortunate."

"That's an interesting theory, Mr. Rodriguez, but can you prove it?"

"Sure I can. Just look at low income housing, for example. For the last fifty years, your politicians have been paying lip service to "housing for the poor," and have invested large sums of taxpayer dollars into providing low rent housing for them, built by rich billionaire slumlords, of course, who were only happy to take the government money. The results were just more slums.

"Then, after your housing projects failed, you started messing around with the housing market by guaranteeing mortgage loans. From a politician's point of view, government guarantees were a cheap way of buying votes. It doesn't cost anything – that is, until there are large loan defaults."

"I think you're onto something, Mr. Rodriguez. Ms. Baxter, I see you're raising your hand. Do you care to weigh in on this?"

"Yes, I do. Whenever you guarantee a loan, you also open an opportunity for a capitalist to figure out a way to profit from the guarantee. Anyone who knows anything about investing knows that the higher the risk, the higher the expected return. Before we knew it, Wall Street was offering securities based on these 'guaranteed' loans."

"That's right," added Carlos. "Whenever you start out offering a situation without risk, you attract the attention of Wall Street and the financial services industry. Banks, for example, under the Glass-Steagall Act, were prevented from getting into the housing finance business. For years, banks lobbied to have this restriction removed and, after twenty years and some $300 million later, they succeeded. The $300 million they spent bought the votes they needed to repeal the legislation."

"Are you saying that our political system is corrupt, Mr. Rodriguez?"

"It's a matter of public record – just log on to the web site that keeps records of campaign contributions and see the paybacks for lobbyists. Even the former chairmen of Citicorp said that Glass-Steagall protected the economy. "

"What about the rules that the FHA has when guaranteeing housing loans?" Bob asked.

"For the seller of housing the government guarantee costs ½% of the loan and for the 20% down payment the builder just jacks up the cost of the house and adds it to the selling price. Didn't cost the buyer anything. In fact it was cheaper to buy a house than rent one."

"Mr. Brammon says that regulation can get us out of it. So, is it more regulation that we need, or less of it?"

"I think we do need a Constitutional amendment to take the profit out of politics by imposing term limits," said Snookie.

"But isn't it true that nothing happens in a Congressman's first two years?" asked Ike.

Harry stepped in. "Under the good-ole-boy system, maybe. But if they all served for the same terms, there wouldn't be such a buildup of power by a handful of people. And it wouldn't be profitable for big business to contribute to them.

"Don't you think we also need legislation to limit campaign contributions and to prosecute politicians who use their political position by breaking our laws?"

Snookie raised her hand. "Of course. Politics should be a field that attracts statesmen, not future CEO's and board members. Almost everyone in politics nowadays has at least one conflict of interest."

"Well, we have a lot to think about the problems and the causes, class. But be ready tomorrow to also discuss possible solutions."

"He doesn't ask for much, does he?" asked Ike as he and Snookie packed up their books. Snookie looked at Ike with absolutely no expression.

"Ike Pendleton," he said, reaching out with his hand. Snookie took it firmly, like a man, as she said, "I know who you are. Professor Mason introduced everyone."

"That's some shake you have there. I just wanted to make a more personal introduction."

"I don't date fellow students," Snookie replied, and she turned and walked away.

Carlos nudged at Ike with his elbow as he walked up the aisle to the exit.

"Dude, did you get moded!"

CHAPTER SEVENTEEN THE SIMPLE THINGS

.

When traffic came to a standstill, Ike and Snookie decided to get off the highway and try to find gas. It used to be easy. Stop into a gas station, which you could find on almost any block, gas up your car, and step inside to grab some snacks in the mini market. All of that had changed. The first challenge was to find a station that had power and was open. When they finally did, there was a line. The Government hadn't even had the chance to impose rationing yet. And the price was subject to fluctuation as you waited in line.

Ike and Snookie pulled in behind a line of cars waiting two blocks ahead of a large filling station. After about an hour of waiting, the station put up a sign, Out of Gas. Then all hell broke loose.

First, there was an orchestra of horn honking. Then, several cars screeched out of the line and peeled off down the road. At the front of the line, it was even worse. At the front of the line, a big man, wearing a tank top which exposed huge biceps covered with tattoos, protested.

"I've been waiting here for over two hours. You can't be out of gas!"

He ran to the double glass doors of the station, which were locked, and pounded on them, furiously.

"Open up! You've got a whole mini market full of stuff in there!"

The man banged harder on the doors, and the terrified Indian clerk inside cowered behind the counter.

"You god damned sand nigger! Turn the pumps back on and open up the store!"

The man's anger was building to a crescendo. He paced back and forth in front of the store, swearing. Then, he hammered on the on the window again. Finally, he ran to his pickup truck, got in, fired it up, and drove it head on into the store, crashing through the glass. He jumped out of the car and Ike and Snookie heard a series of shots.

Ike got out of line and accelerated away.

"We've got to get out of here!"

"Is it really worth risking your life for a tank of gas or bag of potato chips?"

"I guess, if you're hungry enough. You saw yourself. There was a run on the markets. And when they ran out of food, the people wouldn't accept it, so they just tore them apart."

***

As they approached the outskirts of Gary, Indiana, the plumes of smoke that used to belch from the smokestacks of the factories had been replaced by clouds of smoke from a city that was burning. Gary had always been kind of run down, but now it looked like a war zone. Armored vehicles from the National Guard patrolled downtown. Police fought off rioting crowds in the center, using water cannons and tear gas. Ike and Snookie looked outside at the horror, as they searched for an open gas station. As soon as he found a safe place, Ike pulled over. They had come to a crossroads in the beginning of their journey.

"Looks like nothing's open here, either. Better get back on the road."

Ike looked at the map.

"We can either go south on the 65 to the 70, through Indianapolis and Columbus, or north on the 90, through Toledo and Pittsburgh."

"What's better?"

"Your guess. They're probably both bad. The southern route is 60 miles more, so we'd burn less gas on the northern, if we have gas. It also goes through Indianapolis. We should probably avoid the big cities. They're probably worse than Gary."

"I guess we go the northern route, then."

CHAPTER EIGHTEEN HARRY'S WORKSHOP

Harry worked on his index cards in his study, while Jennifer played with Jackpot.

"What's Cramer saying today, Jackpot?"

"Market is down. Cramer says buy!"

"Harry, does he actually understand what Cramer is saying, or just repeats his phrases?"

Harry looked up from his cards, appearing perturbed.

"What?"

"I'm sorry, Harry, I didn't mean to interrupt you."

Harry paused and put the cards down. The most important person in my life, and I'm snapping at her.

"On the contrary, dear, it is I who am sorry. What were you saying?"

"I was saying, does Jackpot really listen to Cramer, or is he just repeating phrases he likes?"

"Oh, I'm sure he listens. In fact, Jackpot has as good a chance to beat the market as any top broker in any of the big investment banking firms."

"Really?"

"Of course. They don't know any better than Jackpot. Or Cramer, for that matter."

"Cramer says buy!"

Jackpot ruffled his feathers, and started making "door knocking" noises.

"Someone must be at the door. I'll get it."

Jennifer went to answer the door and Harry went back to his index cards.

"It's Mr. Rodriguez."

"Show him in."

Carlos Rodriguez walked into Harry's office just as he was hiding his index cards.

"Cramer says buy!"

Jackpot nodded his head up and down, furiously. Carlos motioned to the bird with his thumb.

"Hello, professor. Cramer?"

"Everyone asks me about that. Have a seat, Mr. Rodriguez, and meet Jackpot, Jim Cramer's biggest fan."

"Hello, Jackpot."

"Hello, Jackpot."

"He's cute. You should introduce him to Ike's monkeys."

"I'm afraid Jackpot has no time for monkey business. Now, what's on your mind, Mr. Rodriguez?"

"I'm having a struggle with my thesis on free market capitalism."

"What's your quandary?"

"My hypothesis is that a true free market system will work, but I can't find any models for it."

"You won't. There aren't any."

"None?"

"None. Supporters of pure capitalism, such as you, Mr. Rodriguez, argue that only a free market can create healthy competition, fostering more business and reasonable prices."

"Yes, yes, it can. But I need to show that."

"The critics are against you on that. They point out that, when companies are truly free from market regulation, they grow and form monopolies, which, in turn, requires government regulation to force competition and reasonable prices."

"So, you're saying that a free market system won't work?"

"On the contrary, I believe in some type of free market system. I just don't think you'll find an example of one completely free from government intervention."

"And when you mix government and the economy, you get interference from politicians."

"Politicians are crooks!"

"Well put, Mr. Rodriguez, and you too, Jackpot."

"You too, Jackpot!"

"With our current political system of lobbying, you get lopsided government regulation."

"Like deregulating the banks, and then regulating the currency, which inadvertently forces the banks into other investments."

"Yes, and by loaning them money for no interest, you're really letting them into the casinos with the house's money, aren't you?"

"House's money!"

"I see what you mean. Giving the banks free interest loans is like the government subsidizing the banks. That's loco, man!"

"Now you've got it, Mr. Rodriguez. And I think it may be useful for our Washington project."

"Do you really have an invitation from the Senate Finance Committee?"

"Yes, I do. They've been known to call on me from time to time. Especially when they're in trouble."

CHAPTER NINETEEN GETTING TO KNOW YOU

Ike looked out the window at the plumes of smoke on both sides of the interstate. It had been over an hour and they had not said a word to each other, so he tried to stir up some kind of conversation.

"Where are we now, Snookie?"

"According to this map, we're just south of Cleveland, and north of Akron, my home town."

"I didn't know you were from Ohio."

"Yeah."

"What was it like, growing up in Akron?"

"What do you mean?"

"I mean, did you live there up until you went to school?"

"Yeah, I did my undergrad at UChicago, too."

"What did you major in?"

"Mathematics."

"So Akron, then Chicago?"

"Yeah."

"Tell me about your life, your boyfriends."

"Didn't really have any. I went to a specialized school."

"For gifted kids, I bet."

"Something like that."

"What do you like to do?"

"Do?"

"Yeah, do you have any hobbies?"

"Why do you want to know so much?"

"Just interested, is all. Don't you want to know my hobbies?"

"Not really."

Ike suddenly felt awkward and strange.

Six hours or more to go and nothing to talk about.

"Tell me about yours."

"My what?"

"Hobbies."

"I like to read."

That's a good start – literature.

"Great! Do you like the classics? I like Dickens and Steinbeck."

"I didn't really do well in English. I'm more of a non-fiction reader."

"Like what? Politics?"

"Mostly economics. I pretty much remember everything I read."

"I noticed. Do you like any games?"

"I can play cards."

"Really? What kinds of card games do you like to play?"

"Anything, really. I can remember all the cards."

"What do you mean, all the cards?"

"I just remember which cards are played."

"Remind me to take you to the blackjack table sometime." Ike smiled, but Snookie showed no reaction to his humor.

Okay.

"I'm pretty good at chess, too."

"Oh, you like to play chess?"

"Not really. I'm just good at it. I read a couple of books on master chess moves and pretty much know all of them."

"What about movies? Do you like movies?"

"They're okay, I guess. But they give me bad dreams, sometimes."

"Why?"

"I don't like the scary parts. They play back over in my mind."

I guess I won't ask her out to a film.

"Maybe, when this is all over, we can get together and go out sometime."

"For what?"

"For a nice dinner, maybe."

"I don't get very hungry at night. Mostly at lunchtime."

"Then, maybe for a nice lunch."

Ike smiled warmly, but got no reaction from Snookie.

CHAPTER TWENTY GREED

Harry stood in front of the class, with two attractive women on each side of him – his wife, Jennifer, and June Lockheed, the registered investment advisor.

"As promised, today I would like to present to you two experts. The first is my wife, Jennifer Mason, an economist who has published articles on complexity economics. The second, June Lockheed, a registered investment advisor. Jennifer, you have the floor."

Harry and June sat down and Jennifer took center stage.

"Does anyone know the concept of complexity theory as it applies to economics?"

Snookie raised her hand. "Yes, young lady?"

"Complexity theory is sometimes called complexity systems theory. It's the concept that certain systems have many different components that interact with each other in different ways."

"Very good. Is there anyone who can think of what the implication may be with economic systems, such as the stock market?"

"Well, for one thing, there's the human factor, which we can't overlook."

"Very good, Mister?"

Harry interjected, "Mr. Pendleton is an expert on neuroeconomics."

"Good, Mr. Pendleton. That's one element, but the point is that economic systems can't be looked at in a vacuum. There are too many factors that come into play that makes them a complex system. For example, how does greed come into play?"

"We know we're in another stock market bubble, and another housing bubble, but the large institutions continue to trade in derivatives, to make money for money's sake," said Ike.

"That's correct, Mr. Pendleton. Warrant Buffett called derivatives 'financial weapons of mass destruction,' and they're one of the reasons why the market must be considered a complex system. Because our economy is also a complex system, we have to look at the gross notional value of derivatives that are the mainstay of the "too big fail" banks' investment portfolios.

"That gross amount is over 800 trillion dollars, which is more than ten times the worldwide gross domestic product. Because you can't look at the market on a linear scale, you have to assume risks on a non-linear or exponential basis. Therefore, a failure of the large banks would take the entire world economy down with them."

"But isn't it normal for banks to look for alternate ways to make money since the Fed is holding interest rates down so low?"

"Yes, but the problem is that the banks are too big. One of them goes down and the rest follow like dominoes, crippling the entire monetary system. These banks got as big as they are by acquisitions and mergers. We don't need them to be so big. In fact, it is detrimental to our economy."

"So the solution is to break up the big banks?"

"As I said, we don't need them. Smaller banks can always syndicate together for large financings, and if one or a few of them fail, it won't destroy the whole system. Breaking them up is one solution, but also a political conundrum. The financial elite already have the politicians in their pockets, as a result of their lobbying."

"I call it legalized bribery," said Harry.

"I think you're not going to see a breakup anytime soon, unless of course, there is an entire systemic failure, and then it will be too late."

"What will happen then?" asked Larry.

"Something else will replace the dollar as the world's reserve currency."

"Like what? Gold?" asked Bob.

"Gold, maybe. It's been referred to by some financial experts as the only real money in the world. And when you see central banks like China and Russia stockpiling it, you can bet that they are hedging for this possibility."

"What else, besides gold, I mean?" asked Carlos.

"The IMF can issue its own fiat currency, SDR's, which have been used already to bail out economic crises in Iceland, Greece and Cyprus."

"So, you're saying it will all come to a crashing halt?"

"If it does, it will reset, and a new system with new rules will take its place."

"Thank you, Jennifer. That is an example of greed on the largest scale possible. The subject of greed is also a good introduction for our next guest, June Lockheed, a registered investment advisor, who is here to share with us some of the practical aspects of what we've been studying here in class. June?"

June stood up to address the class.

"Thank you, professor. As an RIA, I've come to know greed on a very intimate level. Most of the clients who come to me have already been raped and pillaged, financially speaking, by their brokers. Brokers are, essentially, salesmen. And, just like the used car salesman down the block, they don't care what kind of car you get, so long as you buy it and they can earn a commission."

"But, aren't they required to pass an examination?"

"Yes, but we're talking about a simple examination that basically consists of what they can and cannot say when talking to a client. There are no educational requirements, and most brokers are no more an expert on investments than your local hairdresser."

Murmurs of laughter swept the gallery, and June continued with her story of Tex, the cowboy, and the way he branded his broker to get even.

"So brokers have no fiduciary duties to the client at all?"

"None. Their job is simply to get control of the client's money without breaking the law, if at all possible."

CHAPTER TWENTY ONE A SENTIMENTAL JOURNEY

As Ike and Snookie approached Toledo, traffic on the Ohio Turnpike came to a complete stop. They could see columns of smoke emanating from the glass city.

"What's going on out there?"

"More of the same, probably. See if you can get something on the radio."

Snookie adjusted the radio tuner, which crackled through one static-filled output after another, until, finally, some news.

"The National Guard has mobilized in response to violence on the streets of Toledo. Incidents of looting have created safety hazards for firefighters, as they attempt to quell blazes in city buildings. And scores of fire brigades have been called to battle fires at the BP Refinery."

"Strange they would be burning a refinery, with a gas shortage crisis."

"They don't understand how the huge oil companies could have a gas shortage. No lines of credit, no money transfers, no cash. Everything comes to a stop."

"I see. Ike, there's something I've been wondering about."

"What is it?"

"Why are you studying animals as part of a thesis in economics?"

"It's all part of neuroeconomics. I study how the brain works with regard to making decisions and taking risks. Humans are animals, too. I use animals in my behavior experiments because the experiments can be more controlled and the assumptions of the economic model can be tested better."

Ike smiled. Snookie looked at him, trying to process what he was saying.

"Plus, they're cute, don't you think?"

"Cute?"

"Yeah, fuzzy, furry little bunnies and monkeys. Cute, you know?"

"Yeah, I guess."

"You have to be the first girl I've ever met who doesn't go ape over animals. Get it, ape?"

Ike flashed a goofy smile.

"No."

"Okay, well, forget it."

***

Carlos felt the airplane turning. He pushed the intercom button for the pilot.

"Hank, what's happening?"

"We're being re-routed to Dulles. Ronald Reagan Airport's been closed."

Carlos sighed. Harry smiled and tried to make small talk.

"Well, Mr. Rodriguez, what are your plans after you finish our presentation?"

"What do you mean?"

"Will you go to Mexico before they impose travel restrictions?"

"Travel restrictions?"

"Yes. I assume they will be suspending or revoking passports, at least temporarily. You may not be able to connect with your father if you stay here."

"Will they really do that?"

"At first, it will be international travel. Then, they may impose checkpoints at the state level."

"Unbelievable."

"All bets are off when the elite think they're losing control over the people."

CHAPTER TWENTY TWO THE ABSENT MINDED PROFESSOR

Dr. Reynolds had his office not far from campus. He had been Harry's doctor since Harry had immigrated from the UK. He had been balding since his 40's, which he claimed was a sign of virility – a proven medical fact. Just a few pounds over what should have been his ideal weight, Reynolds was a workaholic, just like Harry, who was about 20 minutes late for his Wednesday appointment.

"So, Brian, what's the prognosis? Am I going to live?"

Instead of laughing, Reynolds looked serious, like a judge about to announce a death sentence.

"We've got the results back on your blood tests and CT scan – all normal."

"I told you I didn't need those tests."

"Well, I gave them to you because of your performance on the memory tests – as a rule out measure."

"To rule out what?"

Dr. Reynolds leaned forward, took off his glasses and looked into Harry's eyes.

"Harry, I think you've got the onset of the early stages of Alzheimer disease."

Harry's mouth dropped open. Alzheimer's?

"But, Brian, I'm not that old."

"Alzheimer's hits people in their 60's, Harry. And, in some rare cases, they even get it much younger."

"Jennifer says I've been working too hard lately on this Government project. It's been putting a strain on me. She said to ask you for something to take the edge off."

"Harry, your blood pressure is normal. You don't seem to be reacting to any unusual stressors. I'd like you to see a specialist. There's a new medication going through trials now. If we can get you on the program, it could help you."

Doctor Reynolds held out the referral slip. Harry took it, looked at it, and hung his head down.

"Well, Brian, if you think I should."

"Harry, I know this is difficult. It's hard for anyone, but for a man with a mind like yours, it has to be the worst news. I'm sorry."

Harry forced a smile. "Thank you, Brian."

***

Harry, faced with the impossible job of breaking the news to Jennifer, didn't know how to spin it, so he just told it to her like Dr. Reynolds had told it to him.

"Jennifer, I think Brian's wrong. I don't think I have Alzheimer's, but I have been slipping up lately in class, you know – forgetting my place in the lectures."

"Maybe you should put an outline of your lectures on index cards. That way, you can refer to them just to keep organized."

Harry made a face. "I've never had to make an outline in my life."

"Things change, dear. I just think it's a good idea. Just in case, you know?"

Harry spent the evening making out 4x6 index cards for his lecture for the following day.

"How's it going, dear?"

"It's terrible, Jennifer. This makes me feel so useless, so old."

"You're neither useless nor old. Everyone has to organize an outline for public speaking. I always have."

"Well, I never have."

CHAPTER TWENTY THREE BE PREPARED

As the Pittsburgh skyline came into view, traffic slowed again, and Ike began to nervously check the fuel gauge.

"If we don't find gas soon, we're going to be in trouble."

"Don't you have an extra can of gas in the trunk?"

"What do you mean?"

"Well, aren't you always prepared for any contingency?"

"Usually not, why?"

"Ike, we've been talking about what would happen in an economic collapse for the past six months, and now we're in the middle of one. Don't you remember anything you learned?"

"Not as much as you, I'm sure. I suppose your presentation for the Committee has been expertly prepared and is ready?"

"Yes, as a matter of fact, it has."

"And you have enough cash on hand to tide you through this crisis?"

"Yes, of course."

"And a little gold?"

"Don't you?"

"I've got some gold fillings in my teeth."

Ike smiled, but Snookie's expression was deadpan. She was like a puzzle to Ike. A super human brain that could recite entire complex mathematical equations, but didn't get the punchline of a joke.

"I was just kidding, Snook. Yes, I've got the basic financial first aid kit, and we used our extra gas back there when we stopped at the gas station. But, if we don't get more gas soon, our stash isn't going to do us much good. We can't run the car on gold."

Ike exited the interstate on a business loop in the outskirts of Pittsburgh. Without gas, their whole mission would be stalled.

CHAPTER TWENTY FOUR TAKING THE GAMBLE OUT

Harry stood in front of the class and panned the eyes of the students. For the first time in his academic life, he had to have his lecture outlined on index cards, so he wouldn't forget what he was saying. He flipped through them as he spoke, and felt a deep depression from the fact that he had to use them as a crutch.

Screw these cards. I'm going to go it without them.

"Who has solved our financial crisis?"

Snookie raised her hand.

"That was quick. Ms. Baxter?"

"Well, I haven't solved the crisis yet, but I will. I've been looking into index funds as an investment for the masses."

Harry smiled. "Tell us what you've learned."

"In my studies of the stock market I've learned that, over time, only twenty percent of the professional portfolio managers of actively managed mutual funds beat a simple total market index fund, and those that do don't repeat in the performance in the following period."

"Further, even those who were fortunate enough to beat the market don't make enough to pay for their services and the cost of the brokerage firm's commission."

"That's an interesting statistic, Ms. Baxter. Does anyone know of any actively managed fund that can beat the index funds?"

Bob Brammon raised his hand. "Mr. Brammon?"

"I know of a broker who's been selling his clients one or two funds for the last ten years that have consistently out-paced the market."

"In the academic literature we find studies that have tested the success of brokers that you've just mentioned. There are over 8,000 actively managed mutual funds today. So, by sheer chance alone we would expect at least one actively managed mutual fund to beat the record. Secondly, you will probably find in this string of success the fund will have been swamped by investors wanting to get in on the success that the manager would have pressed to find enough funds to invest in. Does anyone know how these actively managed funds do it? Ms. Baxter, I see you have your hand up again. What do you think?"

"Most actively managed funds concentrate on an asset class called "value funds" as classified by Morning Star."

"That's correct, Ms. Baxter. Mr. Brammon, I assume that you spent some time in the trenches selling those stocks that your company sells and know what a typical customer's portfolio looks like."

"Well, yes, I have."

"So, class, we have here the opportunity to learn just how one of the largest and reputable brokerage firms works. Mr. Brammon, what if I told you that investing your funds with a broker was no better than taking them to Las Vegas and putting them on the roulette wheel?"

"Wait a minute, professor. Our company has a team of some of the best analysts in the world. And our fund managers are hand-picked from among the most successful in the world."

"Exactly my point, Mr. Brammon. The idea of pooling money together for investment purposes started in Europe in the mid 1800's.

"The first public U.S. mutual fund was called the Massachusetts Investors Trust, and was established in 1924. Today, there are approximately 8,000 funds, the majority of which are sold to the public by full service brokers and investment advisors. Worldwide there are approximately 55,000 mutual funds.

"Why so many funds? They are very, very profitable for those who organize and sell them. Approximately 83,000,000 individual investors own mutual funds. The funds sold by brokers carry stiff fees—usually a sales charge from 5% to 10% of the money invested, an annual operating expense charge of 1.5% and are characterized by high portfolio turnover that cause taxable events, thus reducing potential after tax returns.

"Most investors buy mutual funds to save the time and effort of selecting individual securities for their portfolios and to obtain professional management. The performance of mutual funds is a matter of public record. If you ever find yourself interested in mutual funds, or advising someone who is, remember these simple guidelines."

Harry went to the blackboard and wrote as he spoke. He was feeling vigorous and in control again. *I'll show Brian he's wrong.*

1. Never buy a fund with a sales charge.

2. Never buy a fund solely based on prior performance.

3. Never buy a fund that has been in existence for less than three years.

4. Never buy a fund with a 12b1 charge.

5. Never buy a fund with an annual turnover more than 30%.

6. Use "Business Week's" Mutual Fund Scoreboard to select your fund and look for the highest rated funds with the lowest operating expense ratios.

As Harry put the last period on number 6, he threw the chalk down. Then, he picked up a stack of papers on his table. He looked up at the class, and, suddenly, he felt lost. He scratched his head, and looked back at the papers.

What was next?

"Now, who has solved our financial crisis?"

Harry smiled, but students looked shocked, like it was some kind of a test, or maybe a joke.

Ike raised his hand. "Uh, professor, I think we already covered that question. You know, in the beginning of your lecture?"

Harry paused and looked at the papers in his hands.

"Yes, yes, I suppose we have."

He put the papers down, picked up the stack of index cards, and flipped through them.

"Well, I've made a list of questions that I have on the practices of a typical brokerage company, and for your assignment I would like you to answer each question as best as you know how. Then, when we reconvene, we'll compare our answers with Mr. Brammon's."

CHAPTER TWENTY FIVE ANDY WARHOL

After Ike pulled off the Interstate, he noticed that the needle on the gas meter was dropping dangerously below "E" and was in the red. He didn't say anything to Snookie about it. She seemed nervous enough, and it wouldn't do any good anyway.

After about ten minutes of hoping and praying, he saw a gas station in the distance, and reached the line before he could determine whether or not they actually had any gas.

"There's one, and just in time!""

"Do you know what Pittsburgh is famous for, Ike?"

"I don't know. The failed steel mills, the Pittsburgh Steelers? I think you're going to tell me, though."

"Andy Warhol."

"Andy Warhol?"

"Andy Warhol's artworks are some of the most expensive paintings that have ever been sold."

"What does that have to do with Pittsburgh?"

"Andy Warhol was born in Pittsburgh on August 6, 1928. The Andy Warhol Museum was established there on May 13, 1994. It's the largest museum in the world dedicated to just one artist."

Ike started the car to move up in line.

"How do you remember all this, this – stuff? I suppose now you're going to tell me that this all relates to economics?"

"Yes, Ike. Of course it does." Snookie smiled.

"You smiled!"

Snookie looked at him strangely. "So?"

"That's the first time I've ever seen you smile! So, tell me what Andy Warhol has to do with economics."

"Fine art is a hard asset, convertible to even the strongest of currencies. It has an intrinsic value, as well as a market."

"Yes, I remember Harry's lecture. So, do you have an Andy Warhol, Snook?"

"Yes, as a matter of fact, I do."

"Which one?"

"A Marilyn Monroe lithograph."

Ike pulled the car closer to the pumps.

"What do you like about it?"

"About what?"

"The Marilyn Monroe lithograph."

"It has an intrinsic value."

"I know, I know. But what do you like about it?"

"I don't know what you mean, Ike."

"Why do you like to look at it? What attracted your eye? What makes it special?"

Snookie couldn't think of an answer.

"I don't know."

CHAPTER TWENTY SIX THE PITS

Harry put an outline on the overhead projector. Once again, he nervously shuffled his index cards, making sure they were all in place.

"Today we're going to talk about index funds. Let's look at the record. Over the past 20 years, a simple, low-cost, no-load market index fund delivered an annual return of 12.8%. During the same period, the average equity mutual fund delivered a return of just 10%."

Harry paused, with a blank expression on his face. The class waited patiently, but he just continued to stare into space. The silence lasted for a while, until Snookie spoke to him.

"Professor?"

Harry seemed to come back to life.

"Yes, Ms. Baxter?"

"You were talking about index versus mutual funds."

"Yes, yes, I was."

Harry shuffled his index cards. He had stopped looking at them.

"Over the past 20 years, a simple, low-cost, no-load market index fund delivered an annual return of 12.8%. During the same period, the average equity mutual fund delivered a return of just 10%."

"You said that already."

"Yes, I suppose I did. Repetition is good for learning, you know."

Harry cleared his throat.

" To evaluate this difference, let's compound it over that 20 year period. We find that the average mutual fund underperformed the index fund by 57%. And that's before taxes. The average mutual fund loses an additional 16% to capital gains taxes due to continuous trading. So, as you can see, the average mutual fund captures only 41% of the return the market provides."

Harry looked up from the cards, confidently.

"Now, let's look at how the average investor made out during the last bull market. Hang on to your hats! It's probably a lot different than you would think.

"Most individuals are unable to profitably invest in the market and are left with equity returns lower than inflation. The average equity fund investor earned a paltry 2.57% annually, compared to inflation of 3.14%. by contrast, the S&P 500 index has returned 12.2% average over the last 19 years. The average fixed income investor earned only 4.24%, compared to the long-term government bond index of 11.7%, according to Dalbar's Quantitative Analysis of Investor Behavior."

Harry went back to his cue cards.

"But, the Dalbar study has some flaws that understate the performance of the average investor. A reasonable estimate of investor performance is 4% to 8% below the S&P performance for the period. Therefore I estimate that the average investor returned from 4.2% to 8.2% for the period compared to the S&P index (12.2%) for the last 19 years.

"Most of this poor performance was due to the investor jumping from fund to fund – chasing performance. During this course, we're going to examine an index fund that captures the entire stock market return and add other funds that help to combat inflation and reduce portfolio risk as well. More importantly, we will learn how to avoid the mistakes most investors make. Can anyone tell us who developed the first index? Ms. Baxter?"

Snookie stood up. "The first index was developed by Charles Dow in 1898. He added up the prices of 12 stocks divided by 12 and printed the result in a tip sheet now called the Wall Street Journal. The Dow Jones Industrial Index is a price-weighted index."

"That's correct, Ms. Baxter. That index today is known as the Dow Jones Industrial Average, named after Mr. Dow, who was the founder of The Wall Street Journal. The early issues of the Journal were entirely handwritten, and were distributed in carbon copies. Can you tell us how the index is computed?"

"Yes, professor. A stock with a high price may have more influence in the index than a stock with a lower price but with a much higher capitalization. All other indexes are market value weighted. There are about 430 indexes of equities covering small –cap- stocks, large-cap stocks, and value stocks; sectors of the market such as financials, basic materials, retail, and so forth.

"There are about 30 bond indexes covering segments of the bond market, such as tax-free municipal bonds, corporate bonds, and government issued securities. These indexes are used to evaluate the performance of money managers to see how various sectors of the market are doing and to develop index funds—a fund designed to track the market."

"Right again, Ms. Baxter. Researchers have, over the last 20 years or so, examined stock prices and their returns according to the asset groups suggested by the indexes we have been talking about. By way of an example, it has been found that small-cap stocks have higher returns than large-cap stocks and that they are more volatile; also their prices are more erratic than larger companies.

"The volatility of a security's daily, monthly, and annual prices is a good measure of the stock's risk. A statistical measure of risk is called the standard deviation is accepted by the financial services industry and academics as well.

"Can anyone tell us why the majority of investors do not gain the returns the market offers just by buying index funds?"

Ike raised his hand. "I think I know."

"Very well, Mr. Pendleton, give it your best shot."

"It's because of the avalanche of propaganda circulated by Wall Street and the financial media, both via newspapers, magazines, and television. I can't think of a single bit of news circulated by the media that's of any use. It's how your brain processes this flood of information that creates the problem."

"Do tell, Mr. Pendleton."

"Well, just behind each of your eyes sits a pair of neuron groups called the nuclei. These tiny little structures are most electrically active during the anticipation of eating good food, having sex with a beautiful woman..."

Ike looked out of the corner of his eye at Snookie. Carlos snorted and Ike's face flushed red.

"Uh...or participating in agreeable social activities. Also achieving large, um, financial rewards. This area of the brain has superior pattern recognition capability. It can out process the largest digital computer when it come to recognize and connect a person's face with someone you know and like or someone who has facial characteristics of someone you fear and hate. It also can process by means of its pattern recognition capabilities and ignore the many signals your brain obtains when you are speeding down the highway.

"These tiny little bundles of neurons function without you realizing that they are influencing your actions. They send signals to a portion of your brain called the amygdala, which is the Greek word for "walnut." This area of the ancient brain is associated with feelings of fear. Emotions such as fear and aggression are important for visual learning and memory. At night, when you go to sleep, your brain takes twenty percent of your body's energy to clean up and discard memories that are no longer useful. If you are deprived of sleep you will eventually die."

"I think you're getting off on a tangent, Mr. Pendleton. Are you trying to say that this 'emotional brain' is what causes investors to make mistakes with their investments?"

"Exactly! Think about it. When there's a panic in the markets, what happens?"

"Everyone sells," said Snookie.

"Yes, and when everyone sells, prices go down. That's when they should be buying!"

"Very good, Mr. Pendleton. You sound like the great Warren Buffet's protégé. Well, that's it for today, class. We've run out of time again. But be prepared to continue this discussion when we meet again."

CHAPTER TWENTY SEVEN HALLELUJAH!

Ike took a place at the end of the line, which was actually moving, but slowly. They waited in line for about an hour, and finally made it to the pumps.

"Hallelujah!"

"I never did understand that expression."

"It's when you're so glad that something finally happened, it just comes out of you without thinking."

"How can you say anything without thinking?"

"Snookie, you'd be surprised how many people do. In fact, I think most of what the majority of people say is said without thinking."

Snookie gave Ike a curious look as he exited the car and prepared to refuel. There was a big paper sign on the gas pump that read, "Prepay," so Ike went in to the store.

He came out relatively quickly, gassed up the car, and slid back into the driver's seat with a paper bag.

"Got you some goodies."

Snookie didn't pay much attention to the comment. Ike started pulling things out of the bag, calling out the items as he withdrew them.

"I got some nuts, and some yoghurt, and, oh, I thought you might like these."

Ike held out a deck of cards.

"What made you think that?"

"You said you liked to play cards."

"I said I can play cards."

"Don't you like anything?"

The driver of the car behind Ike began to honk his horn.

"I guess we'd better go."

Ike pulled out and headed down the frontage road, toward the onramp for the Interstate. After about half a mile, they noticed a car by the side of the road that appeared broken down. Outside it sat a woman, about 35-36 and a little boy. There was a man tinkering under the hood.

"Ike, we should help them."

"I'm not a mechanic, Snookie. And the gas station we came from is walking distance for that guy."

"There must be something we can do."

Against his better judgment, Ike pulled in front of the car and stopped on the shoulder.

"Snookie, slide over to the driver's seat and leave the car running, just in case. And stay here, in the driver's seat – no matter what."

Ike got out of the car and walked toward the man.

"Hey, buddy, can I help you?"

The man kept working on his car.

"You got any gas?"

"No, but there's a gas station right behind us, and it's open."

The man whirled around, pointing a gun at Ike.

"I guess I'll have to take your car, then."

The man motioned to Ike with the gun.

"Move!"

The man called out to the woman and her child. "Meg, get Billy and the stuff. We're changing cars."

The woman began to gather their things as Ike backed away from the man, raising his hands. The man kept walking toward Ike.

"Turn around."

"You're going to shoot me for the car? It's not even my car!"

"I said, turn around! And shut up!"

Ike kept backing away on his feet, slowly, letting the man close the distance between them, little by little.

"What if I threw the keys away, as far as I could, before you had the chance to shoot me?"

The man with the gun looked puzzled, confused.

"I'm tired of talking to you. Maybe I should just shoot you now."

The distance between them was becoming smaller and smaller.

"Have you ever killed anyone before?"

"What are you talking about? Of course I have."

The man appeared even more flustered. Ike could see beads of sweat forming on his brow. Ike slowed down his pace and backed against the trunk of his car as the man came closer. He looked back at his wife, who was nervously waiting with the bags and holding her son's hand.

"I said move it, woman! We're taking this car!"

"You know, it's one thing to hit a target on a shooting range. It's entirely another matter to shoot a living person."

"Shut up, asshole."

"You really want your son to see you kill someone?"

"I said shut up!"

As they came closer, the man could see there was someone in the driver's seat of Ike's car.

"There's someone in your car. Get them out, now!"

"I told you, it's not my car. I hitched a ride with this girl."

"I've had just about enough of you. Tell the bitch to get out of the car, now!"

"If that's what you want."

"You heard me. Or would you like me just to shoot you now?"

The man spit as he spoke, and the sweat peppering his forehead poured into his left eye and he blinked.

"Snookie! This man with a gun wants to steal your car. He's asking you to get out of it."

Suddenly, Snookie hit the gas and covered both Ike and the man in a huge cloud of dust as she peeled away. Ike lunged at the man, grabbed the barrel of the gun with one hand, and in a split of a second, struck his wrist with the other hand as hard as he could, as he twisted the barrel, putting pressure against the man's trigger finger until it broke. Then, Ike pushed the man to the ground, pulled the gun away from him and pinned him down.

"I should shoot you now, but I'm just going to take this gun. Now, get out of here!"

The man ran back to his car and his family. Ike looked up and saw Snookie coming back his direction. He waved to her and she swung a U-turn and picked him up.

"How did you know to drive away?"

"You told me to keep the car running, just in case. And to stay inside no matter what."

Ike laughed. "Yes, I did."

Ike's legs were shaking. The effects of the adrenalin injection his brain had given him were still strong.

"Well, did I do it right, Ike?"

Ike smiled. "You did perfectly."

CHAPTER TWENTY EIGHT THE GOOD NEWS

Harry was sweating and pulling at his collar as he and Jennifer sat in the waiting room of Dr. Rebecca Leaver.

"Calm down, Harry. Being nervous is not going to change anything."

"I guess."

Harry's left knee bounced up and down, continuously. Jennifer put her hand on it and steadied it.

"Everything's going to be fine. We'll deal with it."

The door to Dr. Leaver's office opened and she stood there in the doorway smiling.

"Professor Mason?"

Harry and Jennifer stood up and entered the office as the doctor ushered them in and directed them to two chairs in front of her desk. Dr. Leaver looked not too far from 40, had a pleasant smile, and was nicely dressed. To Harry, she looked more like a fashion consultant than a doctor.

"I've reviewed your records from Dr. Reynolds. From what I've seen, and especially the performance on your memory tests, I agree with his diagnosis."

Harry rested his forehead on his hand and sighed. This is not what he wanted to hear.

"Aren't you going to run your own tests, doctor?"

"Have you been experiencing short term memory loss lately, Professor?"

"Yes, yes I have."

"We can put you through more memory tests, or we can talk about treatment. The results of the tests are clear."

"No, no more tests. What can we do about this, doctor? I need to keep my wits about me."

"There are treatments for the symptoms, and also there's a promising new drug in trials right now called EPPS that we should look into."

"Can I get on that drug?"

"First, let's talk about what you're dealing with, and then we'll talk about the treatments, okay?"

"Fair enough."

"First of all, there's no cure, at least not yet. The average life expectancy after diagnosis is from three to nine years."

Harry turned his head away, and Jennifer squeezed his hand.

"Your disease is in the early stages, where you may be experiencing difficulty remembering recently learned facts. As the disease progresses, you will eventually lose your writing ability. In the moderate stages, as the memory difficulties peak, you will lose awareness of recent experiences and events and long term memory, and will have increasing episodes of urinary incontinence. The final stages are marked by personality and behavior changes, the loss of the ability to speak, and ultimately to control movements."

"What's the good news, doc?" Harry forced a smile.

"Alzheimer's is a protein mis-folding disease, caused by plaque accumulation of abnormally folded amyloid beta and tau proteins in the brain. I'll go over what is thought to be the actual mechanisms in a moment, but the EPPS treatment that I spoke about has been effective in that reduces levels of amyloid beta. It could actually reverse the effects of the disease."

"So, what are the chances of my getting in on these trials?"

"Pretty good."

"Then I guess that is the good news, isn't it?"

CHAPTER TWENTY NINE HAPPY LANDINGS

As they flew on, Harry removed a stack of index cards from his briefcase and silently reviewed them, over and over again. Jennifer touched his hand.

"You're going to be fine, dear, don't worry."

Harry smiled at her.

"You've always been as wise as you are smart. And with enough confidence for both of us."

The little plane finally touched down in Dulles after what seemed like an eternity of circling and holding. When they exited baggage claim, it was a free-for-all. Cops in riot gear were moving traffic, and taxi drivers were offering rides into the nation's capital for the unbeatable price of anywhere from $500 to $1,000.

"Don't talk to anyone here. Nobody can help us with anything. Lead the way, Mr. Rodriguez."

Carlos led them to the driver who was waiting for them in a black Lincoln Town Car, which whisked them off to an apartment hotel near the Capitol.

The monuments were dark, but still cast imposing shadows in the moonlight.

"I always loved the Washington Monument, the Jefferson Monument. They remind me of the something special about my adopted country."

"What about the Lincoln Monument?"

"That, too."

"You know, Lincoln was the only president in history to ever declare martial law."

"Don't remind me, Mr. Thompson. I would say hard times call for hard measures, but the Constitution is even a greater treasure than these monuments and the great men who inspired them."

"Looks like our president is following in Lincoln's footsteps."

Out the window, in the stop and go traffic, they saw protestors being rounded up by riot police and shuffled into paddy wagons.

"I'm afraid so, Mr. Brammon. I'm afraid so."

The hotel clerk greeted the group. Carlos checked everyone in.

"We're on the ground floor, just as you asked, professor. They've had rolling blackouts, but this hotel has their own generator for emergency power."

"Very good, Mr. Rodriguez. Tomorrow morning, we meet with the lawyers. Then, we'll take the afternoon to prepare."

"What about Ike and Snookie?"

"What about them, Mr. Brammon? Has anyone heard from them?"

They all shook their heads.

"Then we just have to hope that they're going to get here on time. We can't do this without them."

CHAPTER THIRTY A LOSER'S GAME

Fighting depression was hard enough, but fighting it along with Alzheimer's seemed to Harry to be a battle he just could not win. As he sipped his coffee and sorted through index cards for the next lecture, he put down his cup and the cards and looked up at his wife.

"You know, I love you more than words could ever express, don't you?"

"I love you too, Harry."

"Did you ever think, though, that you got a bum deal with me?"

"What do you mean?"

"I mean, well, we never had children. And I'm so much older than you. And now, this Alzheimer's thing. You must want to turn me in for a new model."

"Harry, don't be silly. Nobody said life was easy."

"But it's just not fair – to you, I mean."

Jennifer looked Harry in the eyes and cupped her hands over his.

"Harry, I'm your wife. We're in this together. We will get you on those clinical trials and we will beat this."

"Thank you, dear. The thought of growing old was bad enough. But the thought of losing my mind is terrifying."

"You won't lose your mind. Your head, maybe, but not your mind. Now, finish your coffee and get out there and give 'em hell, like usual!"

***

Harry ventured bravely into the lecture hall, put his briefcase on the table and arranged his index cards on the podium. This is a detailed one. Here goes.

Good morning, everyone. Do you all remember the question I gave posed to you last week – 'Can actively managed funds can actually beat the market?' Anyone care to jump in on that one?"

"I can answer that, professor. My research in this area is just about finished."

"Go ahead, Mr. Brammon. Give it your best try."

"About 25 percent of them do, but they do it by taking higher risks."

"That's right, Mr. Brammon. As Ms. Baxter pointed out during our last meeting, you can expect to gain higher returns if you take higher risks. But, in the case of actively managed funds, the fees often wipe out the higher returns. Mutual fund companies that try to beat the market argue that it's possible to do so. They are right. It is possible – it's just that those who beat the market this year are not on the list the following year. In fact, it can be shown that the majority of mutual funds just buy value stocks, which are a classification of securities that have low book to market ratio."

"Book to market ratio?"

"Yes, Mr. Rodriguez. The book to market, or price-to-book ratio, P/B ratio for short, is a financial ratio used to compare a company's book value to its current market price. Book value is an accounting term denoting the portion of the company held by the shareholders; in other words, the company's total tangible assets less its total liabilities. The calculation can be performed in two ways, but the result should be the same each way. In the first way, the company's market capitalization can be divided by the company's total book value from its balance sheet. The second way, using per-share values, is to divide the company's current share price by the outstanding number of shares.

"As with most ratios, it varies a fair amount by industry. Industries that require more infrastructure capital, for each dollar of profit, will usually trade at P/B ratios much lower than, for example, consulting firms. P/B ratios are commonly used to compare banks, because most assets and liabilities of banks are constantly valued at market values.

"A higher P/B ratio implies that investors expect management to create more value from a given set of assets, all else equal, and the market value of the firm's assets is significantly higher than their accounting value. P/B ratios do not, however, directly provide any information on the ability of the firm to generate profits or cash for shareholders.

"This ratio also gives some idea of whether an investor is paying too much for what would be left if the company went bankrupt immediately. For companies in distress, the book value is usually calculated without the intangible assets that would have no resale value. In such cases, P/B should also be calculated on a "diluted" basis, because stock options may well vest on sale of the company or change of control or firing of management.

"Active managers often point to Warren Buffett, the famous CEO of Berkshire Hathaway as an example. They imply that since Warren beats the markets that we should believe that they, too, will win. That's nonsense."

Harry went to the board and started to write as he spoke. As he wrote, he referred to his handy index cards.

"Here are three reasons why it can't be true: One, about one-third of mutual funds go out of business every 10 years. Two, about 50 percent are defunct after 20 years. And, three, only about 1 in 3 of the surviving funds outperforms index funds. Surviving funds are the ones that don't close, and it assumes you know which ones those will be, which is not possible. The excess return from the winning surviving funds doesn't come close to the shortfall from the losing funds, and this is before accounting for the losses in the defunct funds before they closed.

"We've addressed one mutual fund versus one index and the low probability for active fund success. But that doesn't define the whole problem because people don't usually own just one mutual fund. They own several funds across diversified asset classes such as US stock, international stock, bonds, real estate, and so forth. Does anyone know what else is wrong with this picture?"

Nobody raised their hand on that one. Not even Snookie.

"Well, I guess you really do need a teacher after all. Even you, Ms. Baxter."

Snookie's expression did not change. She just sat there as usual, soaking up information like a sponge.

"Having several active funds in a portfolio exponentially lowers the probability that the portfolio will beat a comparable index fund portfolio. As more active funds are added, and the longer they're held, the probability that a portfolio of index funds will outperform the active fund portfolio increases dramatically to the point where the index funds have a 99 percent probability of outperforming a comparable portfolio of active funds. Now that's something that all investors should consider!

"Can anyone tell us why active investing strategies fail to beat the market for the vast majority of investors?"

Larry's hand shot up.

"Mr. Brammon, you're on a roll today. Go ahead."

"There are several reasons that active funds fail to deliver, not the least is the cost of trying to beat the markets. Hundreds of thousands of investment managers, investment advisors, brokers, mutual funds manager, pension funds managers, banks, trust departments, individual investors, and traders, attempt to out-fox the markets every day. They spend hundreds of billions of dollars each year trading securities, paying managers and consultants, and buying research. The cost of trying to beat the market makes doing so impossible for most people."

"Very well put, Mr. Brammon. A second reason investors fail to beat the market is due to poor behavior. They seek high returns by looking in the wrong places for outperformance. Active investors chase after past performance, they chase star ratings, and they chase the news. As I mentioned before, the news is already old when you see it. The market has already reacted to it. They're putting money in places today where they should have already had money. This tail chasing game costs investors dearly.

"Back in my day, a chap named Charles Ellis wrote a book called Winning the Loser's Game. Can anyone tell us who Charles Ellis was? Ms. Baxter?"

"Charles Ellis was a leading investment consultant who advocated the use of index funds for investors."

"That is correct, Ms. Baxter. I had the good fortune to meet Charley back in ancient times."

The class erupted with laughter.

In 1975, Charley wrote an article published in the Financial Analyst Journal reporting his study of a number of pension funds that invested in equities. The results floored the financial community. In brief, Charley found that the portfolios managed by the best and highly paid professionals did not outperform the S&P index. Since that time, numerous studies over the last 35 years have consistently shown that selection of individual securities by our best professional "experts" yield results inferior to a mutual fund set up to track an index.

"As Nobel Lauriat William Sharpe put it, 'active buying and selling of stocks by individuals will only run up brokerage commissions and waste time and energy. Turning to a professionally managed portfolio is even worse, according to the efficient market hypothesis, because of the fees required to pay well compensated experts to waste their time.'

"You heard it here, class. One of the best-kept secrets in the securities industry is that security analysis, taken as a whole, does not appear to be either a useful or profitable activity. The reports written by the highly paid analyst working for our Wall Street firms are worthless pieces of paper to promote and sell stocks to the inexperienced investor. One very simple solution to this problem is to buy the entire market. As one investor said, 'Why look for the needle in the haystack; Just buy the entire haystack.'

"Can this be done by the small investor? You bet it can. For example, there is a company called the Vanguard Group, owned by its investors, which has an index fund called the Vanguard Total Stock Market Index Fund Investor Shares. This fund has 3,894 individual securities in it as I write with an expense ratio of only 0.19% and has returned after taxes since inception on April 27, 1992, 10.50%.

"Mr. Ellis made a very good case for low-cost index funds. In the case of mutual funds, the fees aren't the only costs. What other costs do investors bear? Ms. Baxter?"

"There are trading costs, commissions, advisor fees, taxes, 12b-1 fees, administrative costs, research costs and the list goes on. Much of these costs are hidden from investors. For example, most investors in 401(k) plans don't provide investors good transparency on the costs they're paying."

"Yes. Another bastion of gluttony is high advisor fees. This issue is just starting to come out in the media. The typical investment advisor charges one percent per year to manage a portfolio of mutual funds for clients. That's crazy-high given the huge advances in portfolio management software and other technology that have occurred over the years. Advisors today should be able to handle five times the amount of clients with half the amount of staff than they did in the 1990s. These productivity gains have not been passed on to clients in the form of lower fees."

"Then, what should investment advisers charge their clients?"

"Well, Mr. Rodriguez, perhaps Mr. Brammon can answer that for us."

"Well, it's not one percent, which is the 'standard fee' you'll hear in the marketplace. I believe investors shouldn't pay more than 0.5 percent per year to an advisor, and probably less. My firm, J.C. Mortenson, charges only 0.25 percent in annual fees.

We've been charging this low fee for more than a decade, and it has saved our clients millions of dollars over the years. That's real money is in their pockets."

"So, why do so many people try to beat the market if the proof that passive investing outperforms active investing is irrefutable? What is it that triggers their emotional brains to action as Mr. Pendleton suggests?"

Snookie raised her hand. "Ms. Baxter?"

"There's big advertising dollars promoting active management – many more than passive managers can afford. Actively managed funds charge 5 to 10 times the fee of a comparable index fund. Much of this huge revenue stream is spent bombarding the public with nonsense about how active managers can beat the market, and it basically ensures that the truth about passive investing gets lost in the noise."

"Again, right on the nose, Ms. Baxter. Did you know that for every new book published on passive investing there are at least a dozen books published on how you can beat the market? Did you know that for every media interview with a passive investing advocate like myself there are at least 100 interviews with people who claim they can beat the market?

"It's actually amazing to me that any information about passive investing gets to the public, and it's a credit to investors who have looked beyond the smoke and mirrors."

"So what's the solution?"

"The solution, Mr. Brammon, is to start learning the real facts about the markets and investing. Rick Ferri wrote a great book that is required reading for my course. It's called The Power of Passive Investing. Passive investing can usually weather the investor through any storm."

"What about a full collapse of the economy?"

"That, Mr. Rodriguez, may call for some emergency measures. We'll talk about that in the next class."

CHAPTER THIRTY ONE FOR LOVE OF MONEY

"Class, we've talked about the best ways of investing in a volatile market, but we haven't touched on the subject of our money supply. Does anyone here understand how the international monetary system works? Ms. Baxter?"

"It's all about the dollar. The dollar is the world's reserve currency."

"That's right, Ms. Baxter. The dollar is the world's reserve currency and, currently, there is no other currency ready to take its place if it fails."

"The dollar's not going to fail."

"How can you say that with such confidence, Mr. Thompson?"

"Because the United States is the largest nation of consumers. The world needs our buying power. If the dollar failed, they wouldn't be able to sell us anything, and their markets would fail."

"What if I told you, Mr. Thompson, that back in 1978, before all of you were born, the dollar nearly failed as the world's reserve currency."

Everyone in the class looked up from their notes at Harry.

"That's right. The dollar almost failed. Inflation was over 50 percent and the U.S. Government had to issue treasury bonds in Swiss Francs. The International Monetary Fund came to the rescue, issuing special drawing rights, or SDR's, which are, essentially, world currency, until confidence in the dollar returned."

"So, if confidence is lost in the dollar, investors will sell dollars and that will cause their value to drop?"

"Exactly, Ms. Baxter. Economics 101. The dollar is subject to a market like everything else that's bought and sold. Supply and demand."

"Why are we not seeing inflation now, since the Government put trillions of more dollars into the money supply to bail out the banks in 2008?"

"A very good question, Mr. Rodriguez. The Federal Reserve has increased the supply of dollars over 400 percent since 2008 and we're not seeing any signs of inflation. If you accept my premise that we're in a depression, we would have seen massive deflation were it not for the inflationary actions of the Fed.

"But, it's also my opinion that inflation is coming, and, also, that these dollars have not been put to work because the economy is structurally damaged. The Federal Reserve will keep issuing new money until it reaches its inflation target of 2.5%, but that fails to take human nature into account. Perhaps Mr. Pendleton can explain why that's such an important factor."

Ike looked up from his iPhone. "Excuse me?"

"Of course, if you'd rather stay in your phone, you know where the exit is."

Carlos laughed. Ike looked up from his phone, startled, and saw that everyone was staring at him.

"Should we wait until you finish that darling cat video or WhatsApp message?"

"No, no, professor, it's okay. I can answer that. Once we start to see inflation, people will panic and expect that it will go higher. That will lead to even higher inflation."

"That's correct, Mr. Pendleton. The Fed thinks inflation is its friend. If it keeps inflation high, the U.S. debt will stay at a low level, and it can reduce that debt and, at the same time, collect more in taxes. But it is courting with an unsound fiscal policy. If inflation runs away, the dollar will lose its value against gold, and Russia and China, whose central banks have been stockpiling gold, will be there to offer the world a new reserve currency.

"Let's look at the point where we are in terms of history – recent history. From the start of this century, we should have been in a natural state of deflation. The United States is the largest consumer nation in the world and we have enjoyed the purchase of cheap goods from China, made with cheap labor."

"Then, why didn't that put us in a deflationary spiral? Why did prices go up instead of down?"

"The Fed, Mr. Rodriguez. It lowered interest rates, which curbed deflation alright, but it made borrowed money too cheap, which created the housing bubble."

"Then, when that bubble burst, the housing market collapsed."

"Correct, Mr. Pendleton, which turned the spiral back into deflation, this time because of the devaluation of $1 trillion in mortgage loans and trillions more in derivatives based on those loans."

"Which halted construction, increased unemployment, and forced a sell-off of assets."

"I believe that we are in the midst of another stock market bubble, and another housing bubble at this point in time."

"Isn't that good for the economy?"

"No, but it is good for brokers and bankers. That's where the greed factor comes in."

CHAPTER THIRTY TWO FINANCIAL FIRST AID

Harry came in early to class. He sorted out his index cards, and wrote on the board, Financial First Aid Kit. Dean Anderson popped his head in.

"You got a minute?"

"Yeah, Walter. Come on in."

Anderson was the head of the School of Economics. He was about Harry's age, but hadn't taught any classes since going into administration.

"Could you stop by my office after class? I've got some things to discuss with you."

"Sure, Walter. I'll see you – when I've got no class." Harry grinned, but Walter didn't catch the reference to Rodney Dangerfield's Back to School. Snookie and Carlos walked in and took their places.

"Okay, see you then." Dean Anderson left, and, gradually, the seats began to fill in the lecture hall.

Harry called the class to order.

"Class, for a diehard passive investor like me, today's lesson is perhaps the most difficult I have ever had to give. Remember, we were talking last time about a possible collapse of the dollar? I hate to talk like a survivalist, but does anyone have any idea how you would make it if that happened?"

"I do, professor."

"Very well, Ms. Baxter."

"When the dollar drops in value, gold goes up. So, it makes logical sense that gold would be used in place of the dollar."

Harry wrote on the board: 1. Gold.

"How about it, class. Does anyone think that merchants will stop taking dollars and require gold as payment?"

"It would most likely be higher prices in dollars."

"Yes, Mr. Pendleton, but probably just in the initial stages."

Harry wrote down: 2. Cash.

"Well, you're both right. Because our money is digital, any problems in the system would mean that, at least temporarily, cash is king. The investor should keep a six month supply of cash on hand, for a rainy day, so to speak."

"A stormy day."

"Yes, Mr. Pendleton. More like a hurricane. Any other investments you can think of that could weather such a storm? Mr. Rodriguez?"

"Real estate."

Harry wrote down: 3. Real estate.

"Why real estate, Mr. Rodriguez?"

"It's the oldest form of investment. And traditional collateral for modern forms of investment."

"The real estate market fluctuates, as does the market for gold, but it is considered to be a hard asset. Anything else?"

Harry looked around the room. Nobody was raising their hands. He wrote on the board: 4. Fine art.

"Fine art is also a hard asset. If the dollar crashes, you can be sure to find a market for it in whatever money turns out to be the next world reserve currency."

***

Harry fidgeted in his seat in front of Dean Anderson's desk. He felt like a boy who had been called into the principal's office.

"What's on your mind, Walter?"

Walter Anderson looked at him over the straight edge of his bifocals, with a frown. He sighed.

"Harry, you know that I think you've been the greatest addition to the faculty that this department has ever seen."

"Thank you, Walter. But, I'm sure you didn't call me in just to boost my ego."

"No. Actually, we've had some student complaints."

Harry looked up at Walter in surprise.

"Complaints?"

"Relax, Harry. Not from your whiz kids. From some of your undergraduate students."

"I've always told you that forcing art majors to take economics does not compute."

"It's not that, Harry. They say you haven't been sticking to the material in the text. That you seem, well, distant and aloof. Like you can't concentrate."

"Walter, I should tell you that I've been diagnosed with beginning Alzheimer's Disease."

"Alzheimer's?"

Anderson sunk back in his seat, took off his glasses and started to nibble on them.

"Yes, but there's a new treatment I've been approved for that's supposed to reverse the disease, and I can promise you that it won't affect my work. I'm dealing with it."

"That's good, Harry, but, if it's all the same to you, I'd rather take over your undergrad classes until you can report some progress. You can keep your whiz kids class. I know you've promised something important to the Government and I don't want to let you down."

"Thank you, Walter."

"I'm sorry, Harry."

Harry left Anderson's office, wounded in ego and in spirit. It was as close to hopelessness as he had ever been.

CHAPTER THIRTY THREE A WINNING OR LOSING PROPOSITION

Harry's teaching style never incorporated a podium. He didn't want there to be a barrier between him and his students. But, it seemed his new flash card system would not work without it, so he had a lectern installed in the classroom. He stood in back of it, awkwardly, and referred to the first index card sitting in front of him. This will take some getting used to.

"What if I told you that, not only can you not beat the market, but most stocks actually lose money. Would you believe me?"

"I think the statistics are that about 75% of stocks in the U.S. Market have historically generated a loss."

"Based on their performance over the last 40 years or so, that is correct, Mr. Pendleton. Now, if that is the case, why wouldn't investors just stick with the 25% super stocks that are generating all the growth?"

"Because nobody knows what they will be. If you try to compose a portfolio of carefully selected stocks, you could easily wind up with none of the best performing stocks in the market. Missing out on even a handful of these super stocks can be a failure."

"So, if you compose your portfolio by looking for the gems, you're going to go through a lot of turds."

"That's a colloquial way of saying it, Mr. Thompson, but yes. Some investors and fund managers do happen to pick the winners from time to time, but their success is short lived. And, even if you were able to accumulate a concentrated portfolio of super stocks, after a while you'll find that most of your net worth is tied up in a handful of holdings. According to Trim Tabs, there is a trillion dollars sitting in money market funds making next to nothing. Soon investors will see stocks prices to go up and the public will buy high and sell low during the next downturn."

"Which is why I'm saying that neuroeconomics is so important."

"It is, Mr. Pendleton, but, even though psychological factors may cause the market to deviate substantially from its intrinsic value in the short run, stock values still are ultimately are determined by economic fundamentals. The focus of every long term investor should be the growth of purchasing power – monetary wealth adjusted for the effect of inflation. The safest long-term investment for the preservation of purchasing power clearly has been a diversified portfolio of equities.

"There is a fundamental relationship between risk and reward. Stocks that have higher risk will produce higher rewards, or returns, as we call them. The instant a stock shows a potential for increased profits due to a new product, an increase in demand for its products, or more favorable economic conditions, the stock market will react by increasing the value placed on the security. Today each and any change in a company's future fortunes is translated into a movement in the company's stock price. These changes occur at random. That is, they have not been incorporated into the stock's price up to now. This simply means that in today's market all securities and their prices reflect all that is known about the security and the business it competes in. We call this the efficient market hypothesis or EMH.

"EMH is the subject of intense debate among academics and professionals alike. If indeed security prices reflect fully all-available information, then buying and selling securities in an attempt to outperform the market will effectively be a game of chance rather than skill. Thus, risk and risk alone determines the degree to which returns will be above or below average and thus decides valuation of any stock relative to the market.

"I have invented an equation for this called Harry's equation. It goes like this: More volatility=Higher standard deviation=Higher risk=Higher return. Now what does this all mean to the individual? Please listen carefully—the following will save you a lot of money sometime in your future.

"There are no bargains in the market. There is no such thing as a bargain stock. No individual security is any better than any other on a risk adjusted basis, and the market is very efficient at pricing securities on that basis. Further, no one can tell you if the market is underpriced or overpriced at any point in time. Anyone who tells you he has a plan or scheme to find individual securities that will outperform the market for that segment of the market is either ignorant or lying."

CHAPTER THIRTY FOUR LAW IN MOTION

Harry wasn't feeling up to a meeting with the lawyers, so he sent the whiz kids in his place. He briefed them all in his hotel room and gave his final parting words. I feel like Vince Lombardi.

Mr. Rodriguez, what's going on with the lawyers?"

"They emailed over a final draft of the legislation we're proposing. The business center is making copies for us."

"Good. I know how hard it is to read through legalese, but we all have to do it in advance of the meeting. After you meet with them, we will meet back here and have a dry run of the presentations. Any questions?"

For once, there were none. Harry panned their eyes and smiled, proudly.

"You're in charge in my place, Mr. Rodriguez, so don't screw anything up."

"You can count on me, professor."

The group went out to the waiting car, to take them to the lawyers' offices on H Street Northwest. It was a short drive that took an unreasonably long time, due to the location. Finally, the driver stopped at a barricaded checkpoint.

"This is as far as I go, guys. You'll have to do the rest on foot."

"Where is it?" Carlos asked.

"Just down that street."

"Dude, isn't that the White House over there?"

"Yes, it is. That's why we can't move any further."

They thanked the driver, exited the car, and headed into the mob of humanity that had gathered outside the White House. Every conceivable space was filled with people, many of them holding signs.

"This is not a happy group."

"No, Ike, it's not. Let's stick together, guys. We can't fail Harry now."

The police were out in full force. Concrete blocks had been placed on Pennsylvania Avenue, in front of the White House north lawn, which forced the crowd to gather in Lafayette Square. Carlos, Bob and Larry weaved their way through the agitated group until they finally reached the H Street entrance. There, a contingent of police in riot gear stopped them.

"Where are you going?"

Carlos spoke for the group. "We're going to an appointment with our lawyers, right there, across the street."

"Have any proof of that?"

"Dude, I didn't know we were in Nazi Germany. Isn't this the United States of America? Land of the free and home of the brave?"

"Sir, we have strict orders to stop and detain any suspicious persons."

"You mean any suspicious Mexican persons, don't you? We have an appointment with the lawyers, and no, we don't have an appointment card because we flew in for the meeting. But, we do have the fax with the proposed Bill they sent us this morning."

Carlos showed the fax to the police, and they let them pass.

"Good job, Carlos."

"I'm used to taking shit from the police. It's like a badge of courage for a Mexican American."

"It's a good thing we had that fax."

"That, too."

CHAPTER THIRTY FIVE RISKY BUSINESS

Harry stood in back of the podium and flipped his index cards as he spoke. So far, so good. This system seems to be working.

"A broad market index fund contains about 25% less risk than the average actively managed mutual fund. The fact that a portfolio of fifty carefully selected securities will correlate 90-95% with the market's performance does not mean that 90-95% of its diversifiable risk has been eliminated.

"One of the axioms of Modern Portfolio Theory is that current market prices reflect the total knowledge and expectations of all investors, and no investor can consistently know more than the market does collectively. Participants in the market have discounted any known future event so as to correctly price it in today's market. Can anyone tell us how risk and return are related to one another?"

"Ah, as usual, Ms. Baxter, you have the answer."

"Risk and return are related, and riskier assets must therefore provide higher expected return as compensation."

"Mr. Brammon, I see your hand is up. What's your question?

"Well, if what you say is true, then there are no bargains in the market and it is futile in looking for them. Is that correct?"

"But those higher returns are, of course, not guaranteed, or there wouldn't be any risk. But essentially, you are correct. There are no bargains and efforts to find them are futile. I believe that the evidence on the performance of professional stock portfolio managers is proof of this maxim. Portfolios can be constructed that are expected to deliver greatest expected return for any given level of expected risk.

"This is a very important point often overlooked by full service brokers. Either they don't know better or they don't care for their clients but want to maximize their commissions. When one is retired it is only prudent to reduce the risk in your portfolio unless you do not have enough money in your portfolio to live on. Then, you must take a chance and keep your portfolio at higher risk levels. Ms. Baxter, yes?"

"Then, aren't equity markets are far riskier that thought by the average investor and, therefore, a very long investment horizon and the discipline to stay the course are key ingredients of the winner's game?"

"Yes. That's why the biggest danger to a successful investment program is that fellow looking back at you every time you look in the mirror."

The students laughed. "Mr. Rodriguez, I see you raising your hand furiously. Either you have to run to the restroom, which, by all means, you don't need my permission, or you disagree. Which is it?"

"Yes, professor. I disagree. There are market strategies that have been proven to produce returns greater than those of the market and are available to the average investor without any effort."

"Mr. Rodriguez, over the long run, given that, over the long run, the S&P has provided a 10.5% return, compared to a total domestic market return of 10.4%, what examples can you cite of someone beating the market consistently over the same period of time?"

"I can't. I can only point to periods of those who've done it with success."

Exactly. It is virtually impossible to select those stocks that will produce profits over the next 40 years. The numbers I gave you are nominal returns, from which you must deduct 3.5% for inflation. This is proof positive that indexers can and do out-perform the market.

"They use a system that utilize the findings of Harry Markowitz, who developed a mathematical proof that a port-folio of stocks can and will outperform the weighted average of its component parts. I call this 2+2=5.

"A 30 year old should be able to save 12% to 15% of his earned income and have a period of 45 years to accumulate his portfolio and start withdrawing these funds during retirement.

13% of the total will accrue in the first trimester, 27% in the second, and 60% of the total amount will accrue during the final trimester.

"There are no secret or magical formulas to investing in the stock market. Investing is about risk and reward, and choosing the strategy that is most likely to deliver the expected, but not guaranteed, results over time. If I had any knowledge of hoe to create certain outcomes with high returns, I certainly would not be writing about it, as they do. I would be exploiting it.

"Those who obtain extraordinary returns over a few years were just lucky. In fact there is no known way to select those who will be lucky. Is there? A Roth IRA will permit the in-vested funds to accumulate without income tax on dividends or capital gains taxes during the accumulation period or when the principal is withdrawn from the account during retirement. There are income limits and other restrictions when using a

Roth IRA. All assets will be re-priced to current values at the death of one spouse and the surviving spouse will inherit the estate tax free under current tax legislation.

"At the age of 75 a couple should convert sufficient funds to purchase an immediate annuity to produce enough income to cover expenses so that they do not half to sell portions of their portfolio during periods where prices are too low."

Harry suddenly drew a blank, and frantically shuffled through his cards.

"Where were we, class?"

"Returns."

"Thank you, Ms. Baxter. There are two theories about what determines the returns of a portfolio of stocks over the long run. The Wall Street establishment wants investors to believe that it is the ability to pick individual securities and time the market that determines the vast majority of returns. Notice that Wall Street never advertises its success in its efforts to beat the market return.

"A portfolio containing as many as 200 randomly selected stocks can deviate one percentage point on either side of the market's expected return. Although this differential certainly is not significant in any one year, when negatively compounded over long periods of time it can represent enormous differences in accumulated wealth."

Harry referred to his index cards, and started scribbling on the board, excitedly.

"Here are some of the characteristics of a good index: re-balancing and replacement rules should minimize portfolio turnover, a buffer zone between asset classes, the style indexes (growth and value) should not cover all the companies in the index. This eliminates most of the Dow Jones indexes for style. A fund is inherently tax efficient if it has low turnover and there is no loss of from foreign withholding tax credit."

"But what about value stocks, professor?"

"Ah, therein lies the one remaining mystery – that asset class we call value stocks. They provide higher returns as a category, yet when risk as measured by volatility of prices it is lower than we would expect. There are a ton of peer-reviewed studies available to show that active efforts to outperform the market are not a profitable strategy.

"Financial economists believe that the vast majority of returns are not a result of stock selection or market timing skills. Instead, they believe that the vast majority of a portfolio's returns results from the specific allocations to the three asset classes of equities in general, and then, within the equity asset class, the asset classes of small-cap companies versus large-cap and value versus growth companies. Small-cap companies are riskier than large-cap companies, and value or distressed companies are riskier than growth companies.

"A study by Wharton School of Finance at the University of Pennsylvania finds that income annuities can assure retirees of an income stream for life at a cost as much as 40% less than a traditional stock and bond portfolio mix.

"A Goldman Sachs study examined mutual funds cash holdings from 1970-1989. In their efforts to time the market, fund managers raise their cash holdings when they believe the market will decline and lower their cash holdings when they become bullish. The study found that mutual fund managers miscalled all nine major turning points.

"What is one of the first mathematical theorems we learn that relate to this?"

"That the sum of the parts must equal the whole?"

"Very good, Ms. Baxter. Fortunately, when it comes to investment portfolios, this isn't true. The compound return for a portfolio with a fixed percentage invested on various asset classes is greater than the sum of the weighted average of the individual asset classes. This will hold true if the portfolio's asset allocation is kept relatively constant through a program of regular rebalancing.

You can actually reduce risk without a commensurate reduction in by diversifying a portfolio. Conversely, you can increase returns without a commensurate increase in risk.

"The effectiveness of the diversification – the incremental returns – depends on the degree of the correlation of returns, which is the degree to which prices rise and fall at the same time and by the same amount, between the various asset classes chosen to construct the portfolio. Half of American blue collar workers haven't figured out how much they will need for retirement. Nearly one third aren't currently saving for it and those who are have saved less than $25,000.

"During the 1975-1983 period, as the economy was recovering from the great depression, small cap stocks exploded and returned 35.3% compounded. High returns require taking high risks and anyone who offers you an investment that has a good return without risk is a con artist. Over the last 40 years, Congress has acted irresponsibly, taking bribes from the financial services industry. This must stop and we may have to pass a constitutional amendment to establish term limits as Ms. Baxter has suggested.

"The majority of actively managed mutual funds stuff their portfolios with value stocks and are thus closet indexers, so why are you paying someone to buy funds for you when you can buy them yourself with no commission? There are people out there who can beat the market by their skill and knowledge, but to date, no one has figured out how to identify them before they pile up a record of successes.

"Bill Miller, a recent market guru, turned in a record of 15 years beating the market each and every year, followed by three years of failing to beat the market. Of course, the financial press used the S&P 500 Index to make the comparison when his portfolio was more accurately measured by value stocks.

"From 1984 – 2000, 90% of individual investors earned 5.23% on average while the broad market returned 16.2% according to a peer reviewed study.

On study of market timing showed that for 2,000 trading days the market returned 357% but had you missed the 10 best days your return would have been only 7.4% and had you missed the 50 best days your would have had a zero return.

It is not possible to make reliable predictions when the market will rise or fall. If it were possible the market would respond in advance and then it could not rise and fall the way it does."

CHAPTER THIRTY SIX THE BULLS AND BEARS

Harry looked out at the students in the auditorium and felt proud that, despite his memory loss, he had been able to complete the workshop. There was one more lecture, to be followed by more work in the office. He held the stack of index cards in his hands, took a deep breath and started.

"The great bull market of the 1980s and 1990s crashed in March 2000, causing millions of investors to forever abandon the market. Those who did so had portfolios concentrated in a few high-tech stocks and Internet stocks. Similar episodes have occurred in the past as evidenced by Tulip Mania, a Dutch speculative period around 1636. In March 2000, after an 18 year Bull market of absolutely astounding increases in prices, the market crashed and entered the bear market phase that took the broad indexes down by 49% or more and the Nasdaq Composite 78% lower, and to date, although the market has rallied strongly, some stocks have as yet to regain their highs.

"I doubt that investors have, as yet, learned much from this experience. The lesson that you must learn is that the market goes pure crazy from time to time. During the crash that often follows these just crazy markets, you must continue your investment plan without fail. Such a plan should consist of a balanced selection of index funds based on your remaining time to retirement. Properly constructed, such a portfolio will not experience fluctuations as severe as single broad market portfolio.

"At a minimum, the portfolio will have a broad market index fund and a broad bond market fund. The percentage of each can be determined by your age. By way of example, it is often recommended that your allocation to fixed income securities equal your age. A sixty year old would have 60% of his portfolio in fixed income securities and 40% in equities. There are index funds that will do all this for you that have respectable returns over the last few years.

"But, you're talking about a 'regular' market crash, aren't you?"

\

"I don't know what you mean by 'regular,' Mr. Thompson, but this strategy should survive even the so-called black swans, which have crippled the stock market. It seems to always rise from the ashes like a Phoenix."

"But what about a total economic system failure?"

"That, my friends, is something we cannot get through alone. That's why we are going to continue our work on prevention of such a collapse, and present it to the Senate Finance Committee."

The group stirred, excitedly.

CHAPTER THIRTY SEVEN COLONIES IN REVOLUTION

Gassed up and back on the road, although a little lighter in the wallet, Ike was feeling a lot less nervous. As dawn was breaking, they crossed over the Maryland border. Suddenly, Snookie started a kind of speech, as if her "on" switch had been activated.

"Maryland was one of the original thirteen colonies. It's one of the smallest states, but also one of the most densely populated."

"Where do you store all this information? Are you hooked up to a backup hard drive or something?"

"It was a Union state during the Civil War, probably because of the large free black population at the time. Maryland is the state with the highest household income in the United States, as well as the lowest poverty rate."

"I think we'll need a reassessment on that figure, given what's going on now, Snookie. Why don't you see what you can get on the radio?"

She fiddled with the knobs until a station crackled in.

The Government has reacted with caution to the planned two million man march, which activists had scheduled for tomorrow morning. Activists, seeking solutions to the current economic crisis, have arranged to gather in front of the Washington Monument tomorrow morning to protest.

***

As they crossed into Washington, D.C., it looked like a war games exercise. Military helicopters ruled the skies above the city, and armored personnel vehicles patrolled the streets. They stopped at a street blockade, manned by a group of armed soldiers.

"Looks like they're ready for the two million man march."

Ike stopped at the checkpoint and rolled down his window. The soldier looked inside the windows, while his partner walked around the car, checking it out.

"Please state your business in Washington, sir."

"We're attending a meeting of the Senate Finance Committee by invitation."

"May I see the invitation? And some ID, please?"

"Snookie, do you have a copy of the invitation?"

"Of course, Ike."

Snookie reached into her briefcase and withdrew and handed Ike the invitation. She took her ID out of her wallet and gave that to him, too.

"Thank you sir, ma'am. Enjoy your stay in the capital."

Ike drove on. Their GPS was not working, so he asked Snookie to look up the address on the map.

"It's the Riviera Aparthotel on Capitol Hill."

"Here it is. Turn right up here, on First Street, Northwest."

CHAPTER THIRTY EIGHT MOBILIZE

Ike, Snookie, Bob Brammon, Larry Thompson and Carlos Rodriguez sat in the waiting room of Harry's office. All had been the recipient of an unusual summons, asking them to be present.

"Anybody want some tea or coffee while we wait?"

"No thank you, Mrs. Mason." Ike smiled and shook his head.

"Nobody? Well, Harry should be here any minute."

About ten minutes later, Harry walked in with a gentleman dressed in a suit, his speckled dark brown hair showing he had earned his stripes, but was still somewhere short of 50.

Carlos whispered to Ike, "Looks like a lawyer."

"Hello, group. Thanks for coming. I'd like to introduce you to Mr. Kenneth Grant, our attorney."

"Told ya he was a lawyer." Carlos nudged Ike.

"Mr. Grant is going to help us prepare the legislation on campaign and lobby reform and term limits, which will be sponsored by our very own Congressman here in Chicago. He'll be working with each of you over the next few days."

"With us?"

"Yes. Senator Friedling has invited me to make a presentation on the economy before the Senate Finance Committee. I've selected each of you to make a small presentation on your particular expertise before the Committee."

"To the politicians?"

"Politicians are crooks!"

Grant laughed at the bird and he laughed back.

"Yes, Mr. Brammon, to the politicians themselves."

"Politicians are crooks!"

"I can see that your parrot has his own ideas about the presentation."

"Well, Mr. Grant, I can assure you that he is not alone in this sentiment. Now who is in?"

Ike and Carlos raised their hands immediately.

"I'm in!" said Bob.

"Me, too," said Larry.

"Ms. Baxter, what about you?"

"What, what do I have to say?"

"Recite the Declaration of Independence, the Constitution."

"I can do that."

"Yes, I should have known you could. No, I was just joking. You'll be presenting portions of your thesis dedicated to solutions for saving the economy."

"I can do that, too."

"Then, let's get started. We'll break into two groups, and we'll use this office for our work area. Ms. Baxter and Mr. Pendleton, you'll work with Mr. Grant first, so be back here tomorrow at 9 a.m. with pencils and minds sharpened."

Carlos gave Ike a big wink, and Ike flashed back a sour look.

"Next group will be Mr. Rodriguez, Mr. Brammon and Mr. Thompson. All of you should get together and work on your assignments."

"What assignments?"

"How to save the world economy, of course, Ms. Baxter. Any questions?"

Harry looked at the group, who all remained quiet.

"Good, then we'll see you all here tomorrow morning."

***

As Ike left Harry's office with Snookie, he made another attempt at small talk, this time with a purpose. Carlos, Larry and Bob followed close behind.

"So, shall we head for Faba Arabica?"

"Isn't that a coffee shop?"

Ike was taken aback. I thought everyone knew the campus coffee shop.

"Well, yeah."

"I don't really care for coffee."

"Snookie, it's not for the coffee. To study, to prepare our presentations."

"You can meet me in the library in an hour if you want."

"But, we can't talk in the library."

"What's there to talk about?"

Ike frowned in frustration.

"Okay, I'll meet you there."

Snookie parted ways, and Carlos grabbed Ike by the shoulders.

"Shot down again! Dude, you're going for the all-time record!"

CHAPTER THIRTY NINE THE REUNION

The next morning, Harry was pleased to see that his troops had assembled as directed in the lobby. He was even more happy to see that Snookie and Ike were among them.

"Ms. Baxter, Mr. Pendleton. Glad you could make it."

"We're glad too, professor. We almost didn't."

"Alright, we're coming to the final stretch. And, this time, we have to be forceful. The Government will be looking for a quick fix, but there isn't any. They have – we all have – some hard choices to make."

"I've examined your reports thoroughly. You've done very well. I want to thank you all for your contributions."

Everyone beamed back, except for Snookie. She knew they had done a good job.

"This isn't just a garden variety Committee hearing. It's going to be televised to millions of people. So, remember, we have to be informative, but also entertaining."

"Entertaining?"

"Yes. Even in crisis, people need entertainment. The senators are going to try to hang on to their power. And that power depends, not on the rich companies who stuff their bank accounts with cash, but the voters."

"Yeah, and they are one pissed off bunch of people!"

"They certainly are, Mr. Rodriguez, but, ultimately, this is all their fault."

"How can it be their fault?"

"They had the power in them all along to get rid of these ne're-do-wells, but never exercised it."

"So we have to show them that they still have the power?"

"That's right, Mr. Pendleton. We've all learned about what put us in this crisis. Now, it's time to show it to them."

"Show me the money!"

"No, Mr. Rodriguez. Show me where the money went."

CHAPTER FORTY GROUP EFFORT

Kenneth Grant sat behind Harry's desk, dressed in a sweatshirt and jeans, with a mass of paper spread out in front of him. Professor Mason sat in one of the chairs facing his desk.

"I think this is the first time I ever sat on this side of my desk."

"Don't worry, it's only temporary. There's no way I could fill your shoes."

"Nor I yours."

Jackpot made a "knocking" sound and skipped back and forth on his perch, excitedly.

"That must be Mr. Pendleton and Ms. Baxter. I'll be right back."

Harry walked into the ante room and opened the door for Ike and Snookie.

"Come in, come in, you're right on time."

Harry showed them in.

"Hello, Mr. Grant."

"Hello, Mr. Grant. Hello!"

"I see you're informal today, Mr. Grant." Ike nodded to Grant.

"Yes, for the dirty work I didn't want to soil my suit."

Ike, Snookie and the professor sat down in front of Grant and they got to work.

"I have written several drafts here, with the help of your professor, over many months."

"Yes, but we wanted to get your input. You are the young people who are going to inherit this mess."

"Well put, professor. Now, this legislation proposes sweeping amendments to the Dodd-Frank Wall Street Reform and Consumer Protection Act, the Securities and Exchange Act, the Federal Reserve Act, the Lobbying Disclosure Act, the Ethics Reform Act, the Federal Election Campaign Act, and to revive the Glass-Steagall Act, and a Constitutional Amendment limiting Congressional terms. That is a lot for the Congress to bite into. But, so far, the hardest part of all has been thinking of what to name the proposed bill."

"Why not an acronym? Like the PATRIOT Act. Politicians like those."

"Politicians are crooks! "Jackpot squawked.

Harry rubbed his chin. "I was thinking of something more simple, and not deceptive."

"Politicians are crooks!"

"What about the Save the World Economy Act?

Harry smiled. "I like it. What do you think, Ken?"

"Sounds good. Direct and to the point. Now that we have that out of the way, I want the two of you to read over the proposed legislation and, when we reconvene, please let me know what you think and if there is anything you think should be added or edited."

"From the perspective of your areas of expertise."

***

After Snookie and Ike had left with their homework assignments, Carlos, Bob and Larry returned with their own completed.

"Well, Mr. Rodriguez, you're first up."

"Thank you, professor. I've made a few notes, especially on this new Glass-Steagall Act. From a free market perspective, it is my personal opinion that, if the Federal Reserve didn't mess with the interest rates, the banks wouldn't be so deep into derivatives."

"We understand that, Mr. Rodriguez, but we can't reinvent the wheel. This is going to be a lot for the Congress to swallow, even on the deck of a sinking ship."

Grant leaned over the desk. "And we can also expect this to be amended, watered down and eviscerated by Committees."

"I understand, but I think we need to concentrate on limited government guarantees of loans and bank bailouts. We need to break up these big banks, and let them regroup without government assistance."

"I don't that's going to happen, Mr. Rodriguez."

"Still, he raises a valid point. Let's look at his notes, Harry."

Harry nodded. "Mr. Brammon?"

"I think we should require all brokers to be, at a minimum, a registered investment advisor."

"Brokers are crooks!" Jackpot danced on his perch and screeched. Harry laughed.

"That is an excellent idea, Mr. Brammon."

"Yes, but with the powerful securities lobby, I'm not sure it will fly," said Grant.

"What about minimum education, stricter tests for competence, and the imposition of fiduciary duties?"

"We may be able to push that," said Grant.

"What do you think the bill needs, Mr. Thompson?"

"I think we need sweeping changes in the way appointments to agencies are confirmed. The business of revolving door politics has to stop."

"That's something Mr. Pendleton has been working on with regard to campaign contribution limitations. You may want to coordinate with him."

"I will, but my initial notes here emphasize the need for proposed administrators of federal agencies be conflict-free before their appointments can be approved."

"That's a reasonable proposal. I think we can push that one through," said Grant.

"Very good, Mr. Thompson. I knew I picked the right group."

Jackpot made a noise like a key turning in a lock.

"Are you expecting someone?"

"Probably my wife. Jackpot is the world's best alarm system."

Jennifer opened the door and came in.

"Hello, everybody.

"Hello, everybody, hello!"

" Harry, it's late. Haven't you seen the time?"

"I think we'll work through the evening, if that's alright with everyone."

Everybody nodded in agreement.

"But you need to at least break for dinner. You can't save the world on an empty stomach, you know!"

CHAPTER FORTY ONE I HAD A DREAM

As they made their way to the Capitol building, Harry could see that the National Mall was overfilled with hundreds of thousands of people. Outside the Capitol, he saw a perimeter of armored vehicles and heavily armed soldiers and police in riot gear.

The demonstrations had started at 6 a.m., and, despite the line being drawn around the Capitol, the people were present in large numbers. The president had activated the Army National Guard, whose ten units were out in full force.

"We have a history of peaceful demonstrations here, Mr. Brammon. Let's hope we don't break that record today."

People were holding signs, which said: End Wall Street Greed, and We, the People – Too Big to Fail, among others. They were chanting anti-war songs from the 70's.

Harry stopped for a moment to listen to the speakers.

"Professor, don't we have to go?"

"No, Ms. Baxter, we have a little time."

Harry strained to listen to the speaker. It was difficult to do, with the sounds of the helicopters circling overhead.

"Let's get a better place to listen."

Harry led the group through the throngs of people until he could see and hear the speaker better. He was a black man, with a strong, powerful voice.

He sounds just like Martin Luther King, Harry thought, recalling the famous 'I have a dream' speech. The speaker's voice boomed and echoed throughout the mall.

"It is not by accident that we are all in this mess. We, all of you, and I, have lost control of our democracy. And it is our own fault.

"We have allowed this great country – The United States of America – to become for sale to the highest bidder. It is an oligarchy of the elite, who, through their riches, control who is elected to the Congress, the Senate, and the presidency.

"It used to be, when I was young, that the common man had some kind of a small impact on the political process. Sadly, this is no more. Greed has taken over politics, which now has a price tag. It is estimated that, to have a decent run at being elected president, a candidate must accumulate at least three hundred million dollars. Ladies and gentlemen, this does not come without a cost to the integrity of that candidate.

"Candidates for president today have billions in their PACS and Super PACS. And, behind me, in the hallowed halls of the nation's Capitol building, every office is for sale, through legalized bribery called lobbying.

"He's right, you know."

"Yes, professor, and this is just what our new legislation tries to address," said Carlos.

"Every Government office is run, at the very top, by members of the same industry it is supposed to regulate, hand-picked by the oligarchy themselves.

"And now, ladies and gentlemen, you see these armored personnel carriers around me? Do you hear the helicopters circling overhead? The oligarchy is afraid to lose a grip on their power. So afraid, in fact, that they will sacrifice the world's economy to hold on to the house of cards they have created with it. It's time to say NO MORE! No more will we be the pawns of the rich and powerful! No more will we sit on our rights and waste our votes while they plunder our country!"

The crowd began to chant 'no more' in in response to the speaker's fervor.

"NO MORE!"

"NO MORE!"

"God help us if this crowd gets violent."

"No, Mr. Brammon. God help us if the police get violent."

CHAPTER FORTY TWO THE FINAL TOUCH

The days passed by quickly and Harry suspended classes in favor of finishing his whiz kids' sessions with Kenneth Grant.

"I'm concerned with the fact that only a handful of companies control most of the mainstream media. Even the Internet is now being taken over by corporate gatekeepers."

"What's your solution, Mr. Pendleton? We can't abolish the First Amendment."

"No, but we can clean up the regulatory agencies. For example, during the last big economic crisis in 2008, almost nobody was prosecuted."

"The Government goes after the little guys, not their own."

"Exactly. We have to close the revolving door."

"How do you propose we do that?"

"Through term limits and campaign reform."

"I think Mr. Pendleton is right, Ken."

"Well, there you're getting into the same freedom of speech issue. The problem we have with campaign reform is our own Supreme Court."

Ike lifted his eyebrows in surprise.

"While the U.S. was well on its way to becoming an oligarchy, we actually passed a comprehensive campaign reform act in the 70's called the Federal Election Campaign Act. Amendments to the act limited individual donations to $1,000 and $5,000 to PACs."

"What happened?"

"The Supreme Court shot it down in Buckley v. Valeo. Then, in 2002, we were able to pass another campaign reform act called the Mc-Cain Feingold Act, which limited the use of corporate and union money to fund political ads close to elections."

"What happened to that?"

"It was struck down by the Supreme Court in Citizens United v. Federal Election Commission in 2010."

"So the challenge is to craft a campaign reform law that the Court won't strike as unconstitutional."

"That's right, Mr. Pendleton."

"What exactly does the Court find offensive about campaign expenditure limits?"

"Well, in Citizens United, Justice Kennedy felt that they violated the First Amendment's right to free speech."

"Corporations have the right of free speech?"

"Apparently so."

"Are you kidding or what?"

"No. The Court found that corporations who spend money on political ads to advance special interests are essentially the same as the corporations who run newspapers and television media."

"What about the other case?"

"Buckley v. Valeo? In that case, the Court also held that campaign contribution limitations don't regulate conduct, but speech, and, because of that, they violate the First Amendment."

"So, again, spending money to buy a politician is an exercise of freedom of speech."

"In a way, Mr. Pendleton, yes."

"How?"

"The giving or spending of money, say, on a political advertisement, involves not just the conduct of spending the money, but also communication."

"I don't buy that."

"It's not important whether you buy it or not, Harry. The Supreme Court has not changed its mind on the issue in almost forty years. To write a bill they would shut down if we got it passed would be a waste of time."

"Well, doesn't there have to be a balance between speech and controlling corruption in government? Whoever has the most money now can buy any election. And any legislation."

"You're preaching to the choir, Harry. We have to word it so cleverly that it protects speech while, at the same time, deterring corruption."

"What about federal matching funds for smaller contributions?"

"You may be getting somewhere there, but where will the funds come from?"

"Good question, Ken." Harry placed his thumb on his forehead.

"What about requiring equal air or print time for smaller contributors?""

"That may have some promise, Harry."

"Let's work on a public financing plan that will level the playing field. And a ban on federal regulators taking positions with private corporations."

"More likely that a waiting period or "cooling off" period could get passed, Mr. Pendleton."

CHAPTER FORTY THREE THE LIGHT OR THE TUNNEL

The Senate Finance Committee convened under heavy security from the turmoil outside. The Chairman, a plump, greying Senator from the great state of Utah, entered the room, took his position at the top of the food chain, right under the American flag, as if today was just business as usual, and, since the meeting was televised, he called it to order with a self-serving political statement, lasting far too long, knowing that the majority of his constituents would be tuned in to the hearings either in real time or later during the evening news. If there were any solutions coming out of this meeting, he wanted to get all the credit. He acknowledged Harry Mason and his contingent of financial experts, who were seated in the front row, at the tables, in front of the microphones.

"The Committee will hear today from Dr. Harry Mason, the 1990 winner of the Nobel Prize in economics, and his team of experts, who have presented a report to the Committee with their ideas on how to repair the financial system."

Harry was busy shuffling his index cards. Snookie could see that he wasn't ready to begin, so she spoke out of turn to give him time to organize. "I have a question for the Chairman."

Harry looked at Snookie in astonishment, and the Chairman cleared his throat, but, before he had the chance to speak, Snookie dove in.

"I am not sure just why we are here, Senator. You gave a nice little speech, perhaps the best I have ever heard. But we are not here to promote your political presence are we?"

The Chairman furrowed his brows, which were more like grey feathered wings. They matched the grey spurts of hair coming from his ears. He didn't want to appear to be attacking this young woman on national television.

"Let's face the facts. This financial collapse has been a long time coming and neither your Committee nor the entire Congress has done anything to anticipate or prevent it. The banks that each of you gentlemen cater to have been allowed to become too big. Not too big to fail, as you have said in the past, but destined to fail because they are too big. If they were smaller, then a failure of one or even several of them could be contained."

"Now, young lady, I..."

"Let me finish. The brokers working for our largest financial service firms have plundered the average investor's portfolio, ravaged their bank accounts, and have destroyed the lives of our people, while the fat cats in Washington ride the coattails of the oligarchy's money grab. This is serious business and we do not need political favoritism to come between what is the right thing to do. Do we Senator?

"Order!" The Chairman growled and banged his gavel.

"That is what you need! Order!"

Harry was in shock. His mind was raging and pouring out alternative actions to be considered. It all centered on that speech by Snookie to the committee – the words sounded oddly familiar. Harry thought and thought about it. Where have I heard that before?

Of course! They were taken directly from the Declaration of Independence, penned by Thomas Jefferson in 1776. All she changed was the noun phrase subject and the modifiers and objects to reproduce one of the most dramatic sentences ever written in the English language.

"He has plundered our Seas, ravaged our Coasts, burnt our towns and destroyed the lives of our people."–Thomas Jefferson

It now became clear to Harry how Snookie's beautifully crafted little speeches all these months were made up. She was a savant! She was merely retrieving famous examples of well-known and dramatic speeches and altering the noun subjects and modifiers and she sounded very learned on any subject. Her brain was like a computer when it came to memorizing facts – any facts – but she couldn't tell a joke. Now, her skill was put to good use. She was his secret weapon.

Snookie turned to face the crowd in the gallery as they applauded, whistled, and cheered. With a single simple gesture she silenced them and said, "Let's move on with the agenda. I would like to introduce my mentor, Dr. Harry Mason, a Nobel laureate in economics, who will conduct the order and sequence of our report without further interruptions. Thank you."

Harry remembered how Snookie had looked at his mathematical proof so curiously that first day in class. He went back in his mind to that afternoon in the library of the University when he wrote his thesis, all fourteen pages in a single afternoon. Had he plagiarized the formula from something he had previously read? Or did he get that flash of creative genius as required by patent laws. Or even worse, had he made a mistake in the proof and Snookie found it?

Harry stood to acknowledge the Committee, looked down at his cards, then back up at the Chairman and the television cameras, which were all focused on him. *This is it. Sink or swim.*

"Mr. Chairman, and Senators of the Senate Finance Committee, unfortunately, as it has been many times with our government, we do not have the luxury of taking the time to fix our broken financial system because we don't pay attention to it until we have a crisis. But, fortunately we have analyzed the problem and have a set of solutions that will work. Each of you have a copy of our report on your desk, as well as the legislation we propose to save the dollar and our world economy. The dollar serves as the world's reserve currency, and we have the responsibility to our creditors to restore its faith and value."

Harry looked at his cards to keep him on the right path.

"This is not a cyclical problem that we can print more money and throw at. It is a structural problem. The world has become smaller and we need our economic partners as much as they need us. Since it is a structural problem, we need to address the structure of a new world currency.

"There are several ways that we can do this, and still be a leader in world monetary policy. Or we can continue with business as usual and let some other country become the world leader. I would now like to turn the floor over to Mr. Carlos Rodriguez, an expert in economic systems, for his report."

Carlos stood to be recognized, then sat down in front of the microphone, nervously.

"Thank you, professor. Each member of the Committee has before him or her, our report, which shows how, normally, regulation has interfered with the free market system. Government guarantees of loans and bank bailouts have created a disastrous situation for which we are now, unfortunately, feeling the effects. As you can see from our report, you can't have it both ways. You can't give guarantees on loans, and, at the same time, deregulate the banking industry. By allowing them to dabble in other investments, and by keeping their main business of lending money stagnant by lowering interest rates to zero, you have, with this regulation, created a situation where we actually need more regulation to put the economy back into place. Professor?"

"Thank you, Mr. Rodriguez. Now, Mr. Brammon."

Bob stood up in his seat, nodded and sat back down to give his testimony.

"As you can see from our report, the financial industry has been robbing the investing public blind as long as they have been allowed to use other people's money. There has never been proof of any system that can beat the market, yet most brokers tell their clients that they have products that claim to do it.

"That is why we have recommended sweeping changes to the oversight of the industry, starting with national examinations which guarantee competence, and minimum education requirements for brokers. Your lobbyists, and their friends in the SEC will not agree, of course, but brokers must have the same fiduciary duties to the investor as the registered investment advisor. Professor?"

The Chairman was turning pink, and looked as if he would pop from holding back whatever it was that he thought he wanted to say.

"Thank you, Mr. Brammon. Mr. Pendleton, would you please tell the Committee your findings?"

Ike nodded and began his presentation. "The average investor is motivated to make his decisions not only by financial information and advice, which Mr. Brammon has pointed out is so lacking from the industry, but also emotions. That is why it is so important that we take the bias out of the regulators in the industry."

The Chairman interrupted. 'Now, see here, Mr. Pendleton. What bias are you talking about?"

"I'm talking about the revolving door, Senator. You let the securities and the banking industry, and every other industry, regulate themselves, by taking what amounts to bribes from lobbyists. We need to pass legislation to enact term limits and to limit political contributions to take the profit out of politics."

"What evidence do you have of that?"

"For that, I will turn over the floor to Mr. Larry Thompson."

"Thank you, Mr. Pendleton. The problem facing most investors today is the quality of their information. The mainstream media, including the financial media, has aligned itself with the financial elite, and presents a program biased to their liking.

There is also the problem of selective enforcement. When the SEC and the DOJ was called upon to investigate the crash of 2008, hardly any executives were prosecuted. Most of them, actually, were allowed to profit from their fraud and irresponsibility. They concentrated on the little guys and let the big ones go, and this actually decreased the financial elite's competition. This ad-hoc approach to enforcement has to stop. Professor?"

"The first solution has been staring us in the face for years now, and that is a return to some kind of a gold standard. It was JP Morgan himself who said that, "gold is money and nothing else." And we have seen central banks all over the world, such as Russia and China, buying gold as the dollar weakens. We already have in existence, the International Monetary Fund, which has already successfully propped up the Euro with its SDR's in the Greek and Cyprus bailouts. The dollar, or IMF issued SDRs, could serve as the world's reserve currency, collateralized by gold reserves, the majority of which are already held in Europe and the United States.

"But this is only a part of our recommendation. We must enact legislation to regulate the almost unregulated trading of derivatives. The notional value of derivatives traded in the market every year is over ten times the size of the world's economy. And we need to return to sensible bank regulation. Banks cannot be aggregated in the hands of so few, so that the failure of one or two of them causes a failure of the entire monetary system.

"Finally, and this will be of extreme interest to you gentlemen, you need to realize who your bosses really are. They are the voters, whose savings have been stolen and destroyed by the negligence and greed of your benefactors. It is time for sensible term limits to be imposed and limitations to be put on political contributions. We need to show the Congress that our Government is no longer on sale to the highest bidder. It belongs to the voters."

"Professor, I resent that implication."

"Senator, it's not an implication. It's a fact. Ms. Baxter, could you enlighten the Senator, please?"

Harry knew that Snookie, the human encyclopedia, had memorized the Senator's voting record and could spit out the statistics in a way that not even he could recall.

"Your voting record, Senator, shows that you have voted against the Bring Home Jobs Act. It also shows you voted no on the Protect Women's Health from Corporate Interference Act and voted against funding Planned Parenthood. You pride yourself on being 'green,' yet you've voted against carbon pollution guidelines consistently across the board.

"You voted against the Student Loan Affordability Act and in favor of the wars in Iraq and Afghanistan. You voted in favor of the largest defense spending bill in United States history, voted to extend the Patriot Act, voted no on the Dodd-Frank Wall Street Reform and Consumer Protection Act, no on the Medicare Bill, and in favor of the big bank bailouts. Does that pretty much sum up your accomplishments? I would say that it is pretty clear who you work for, and it's not the voters of the United States of America."

Harry stood up to finish. He looked right into the television cameras, and did it without his index cards.

"The choice is clear, Senators. Printing money to bail out the big banks is not going to work this time, and, if you do it, you will be contributing to the collapse of the international monetary system, and signing the death warrant for the dollar. The people have spoken. We recommend that you pass the legislation that has been prepared for you and sitting on your desks. We've named it the Save the World Economy Act because that's exactly what it has been designed to do. All you people out there need to do is to pick up the phone and call your Congressman now. If you can't call, then email. Tell him that you're tired of business as usual in Washington and that you the Congress to do the right thing and pass this bill."

The audience gave Harry and Snookie a standing ovation, much to the chagrin of the Committee members, who were, themselves, supposed to be representing the people. Harry turned to Snookie as they walked out.

"Well done, Ms. Baxter. Thanks for helping me in there."

"Birds of a feather will flock together, professor."

Had she sensed that I, like her, had a mental deficiency?

"Excuse me?"

"William Turner, 1545, The Rescuing of Romish Fox."

For once, Harry thought he noticed a gleam in Snookie's eye. He smiled back at her, understanding the proverb but not the source. He was sure, however, that it was accurate.

"Of course. Well, hopefully enough people have seen our performance and flock together so that these gentlemen have no choice but to do the right thing."

Harry walked out of the hearing room, hand in hand, with Jennifer, and with his team of whiz kids at his side. They had done their part to save the world. Now, it was up to the people.

AFTERWORD

My father, Gordon L. Eade, is the only man I have ever known who was able to retire at the age of 53 and live entirely off of his investments. He did this with a "buy and hold" policy that saw him through the 1980's recession, 1987's Black Monday, the savings and loan crises, the 1990's recession, the Dot Com Bubble, and the Financial Crisis of 2007-2008. His comments, which follow mine, tell you everything you need to know about his strategy, and, of course, they are inextricably intertwined within the story.

I am a writer of fiction, not a financial expert. However, the research I have done for this book has led me to believe that the bubbles that we are currently sitting on top of call for preventative measures. I believe that the black swans my father weathered with his method will pale in comparison under the scenario of a full monetary collapse, the likes of which is described in the story.

I suggest, as further reading, James Rickards, The Death of Money (The Coming Collapse of the International Monetary System). Mr. Rickards prescribes an actively managed portfolio of 20 percent (physical) gold, 10 percent fine art, 30 percent cash, and 20 percent alternative funds, such as hedge funds and private equity funds, particularly those which involve hard assets, energy, transportation, and natural resources (some of the types of funds recommended by my father.)

One more thing...

I hope you have enjoyed this book and I am thankful that you have spent the time to get to this point, which means that you must have received something from reading it. If you believe your friends would enjoy this book, I would be honored if you would post your thoughts and also leave a review.

Best regards,

Kenneth Eade

info@kennetheade.com

BONUS OFFER

Sign up for paperback discounts, advance sale notifications of this and other books, and free stuff by clicking here:

http://www.kennetheade.com/free-download/

I will never spam you.

***

I have been an investor in marketable securities since I was 10 years old. That was 77 years ago. My first investment was to purchase some postal savings bonds. I had saved up a dollar and bought my first bond that paid 2 1/2% per annum from at the post office.

After serving in the Air Force (I was drafted after the war was over,) I decided to use my education benefits and go to college. I joined the student body of a brand new all men's college that copied the curriculum of Harvard's graduate school's MBA program.

We used the very same books and several Harvard full professors were on the staffs who were lured to California with a three hour a week teaching load and free rent in single family home in sunny California.

So, in effect, I received the equivalent of an MBA degree at no cost with my GI benefits.

After graduating with honors I was placed by the college in a bank as a trainee. My first memorable experience was when a federal bank examiner challenged my practice of taking morning coffee. You may think, how could I get in trouble drinking coffee? Well, the teller's window I manned cashed municipal bond coupons, processed trade acceptances, and accepted payments on promissory notes. It was my daily practice to go to the chief cashier and with draw $15,000 for my cash drawer and go next door for my morning coffee before the bank opened for business. When I returned there was someone at my cash drawer placing a seal on it. The gentlemen asked who I was and I said, "This is my post. Who are you?" He answered that he was a federal bank examiner and wanted to know where I had been. I told him I was getting coffee next door at Manning's Coffee Shop. Then, I opened my cash drawer and put the cash in its proper place. The bank examiner then said that the bank's money does not drink coffee and wrote the incident up in his audit report. After this and many other equality other embarrassing episodes, like falling asleep one afternoon in an area that was provided for those not feeling well, and throwing the bank out of balance several times, I decided that I was not going to be a success as a banker. My employer agreed.

My next job was working for the Grande Oil Company, a subsidiary of Gulf oil located in Maracaibo, Venezuela as an accountant. I was placed in charge of a staff of fifty or more local

Spanish speaking Venezuelans working in the area of accounting for plant and equipment.

We calculated deprecation of physical equipment, based on physical life and the amortization of intangible drilling costs based on recoverable oil in each field and producing sand. By massaging these figures I could report just about any profit number needed, including the government's share of the profits. The government had already taken most or their entire share of profits via customs' duties. So the game was to come out even and adjust the books so that the prepaid customs duties exactly matched the reported profits. Of course, the government had already spent their share by changing the depletion allowance by changing recoverable oil estimates and either physical life of equipment or its economic life. I soon became an expert cooking the books.

After my experience abroad, I joined U.S. Steel as a computer programmer, where I learned their standard cost system, the most advanced system devised at the time. Five years later, I was recruited by U.S. Borax and Chemical to set up a standard cost system for their mine and refinery in Boron, California, site of the largest borax mine in the world.

Other challenging jobs I held were consultant to the government of Greece on industrial development, working with the staff of Aristotle Onassis, the design and installation of an automated oil field in Sumatra, and even the design of the Apollo reentry backup system, among many other projects. My last job was Treasurer and member of the board of directors of a public company listed on the AMEX.

After doing S-1 registrations, tender offers, acquiring several other companies, defending the company from shareholder lawsuits, negotiating labor contracts and firing the company's auditor and solving a ton of other problems, I sold my unregistered shares in a tender offer and retired at the age of 53.

Early on, my buddies, with our new PC's (when they first came out from IBM) were trading on the NYSE using our computers to enter orders directly to the floor of the exchange. In the early days, no one was watching us and, at times, we were not too accurate in meeting the five day settlement rule to settle our accounts.

Sometime in the 1970's I jumped into the bond market after reading Fabozzi's handbook of fixed income securities. At the time, long term treasury bonds were yielding 14%, zero coupon municipal bonds 12%, and listed telephone bonds were yielding 18%. I leveraged the portfolio to the extent possible so that the interest income just paid for the margin costs.

At the peak of this foolish, risky venture my debit balance was way over $580,000. This was a non-deductible expense because of the municipal tax free bonds. I did, however, have an exit strategy. Over time, the interest income paid off the margin debt. As interest rates declined the value of the bonds sky rocked to unreal values. Foolishly, Ii liquidated the bond portfolio prematurely and took the profits.

The lesson I wanted to impart from this book was how to invest in the stock market and to leave you with some things that you should consider before you make a decision about selecting any investment. The more you know about the stock market, about the history of investing in capital markets going back for the last 5,000 years, the better you will be prepared to make correct investing decisions.

As a rule of thumb, it is extremely unlikely that there is, at any moment in time, any bargains in the market. The market is extremely efficient and temporary bargains last only a few seconds in today's markets. Highly paid experts with resources we can only dream about are watching the market closely, seeking opportunities to buy at favorable prices, which is not to say that the market does not go crazy at times, but you know that is occurring by when watching the VIX warns you in advance by soaring well before euphoria hits the market.

The more you know about the people you will encounter in the financial services industry, and, I might add, about yourself and about those three pounds of grey matter up there encased in your skull that can cause you to unconsciously make damaging mistakes, the better off you will be. It boils down to understanding the limbic system, that portion of your ancient brain that protected you from being eaten for dinner by a hungry saber tooth tiger.

Early on as a child, I'm sure you watched your mother make a batch of tollhouse cookies. She mixed some flour with butter, sugar, and baking soda, in the right proportions, added some chocolate chips, put the mixture in the oven and a new product came out of the oven. A product that tastes entirely different from any of its individual ingredients.

Well believe me, portfolios of securities work in exactly the same way. If I take a selection of individual stocks and bonds organized into groups called asset classes, I can create a portfolio of securities that will have an expected return higher than the weighted average of its component parts with significantly less risk. If you had told a Wall Street executive that you could buy a sample of the entire domestic market in a single transaction without paying a commission he would have jumped out the window.

Be sure to open up a Roth account and place the maximum amount into the account in each year. For those under 50, you can contribute up to 5,500 per year and at the age of 60 $6,500 per year.

Modern portfolio theory

A young graduate student named Harry Markowitz in wrote his PhD thesis, which consisted of just a number of equations, in one afternoon in the library of the University of Chicago one afternoon, or so the story goes. His doctoral thesis was all of 14 pages long. His two professors immediately recognized the importance of the discovery, but took a few minutes to figure out whether the degree was to be in the field of mathematics or economics.

Unfortunately, to populate the equation with the appropriate values, we need to know the expected return of each and every security in the market, an expression of their risks and the relationship of each security to one another. This task cannot be accomplished within the life expectancy of a human being on the planet in which we live or computed with the fastest computer we know of today after obtaining the data.

The solution was to assign each security to one of several asset classes based on the size of the company measured by its market capitalization, and its risk as measured by the volatility of its prices, and by its correlation with all other asset classes. Later (in 1990) we added another asset class called "value stocks," identified by the ratio of stock price to book value per share.

As the story goes, in 1953 Harry Markowitz wrote his thesis in one afternoon in the library of the university of Chicago and years later was awarded the Nobel Prize in economics along with William Sharpe. For the first time someone linked risk to return. Simply stated – a Markowitz efficient portfolio is one where no added diversification can lower the portfolio's risk for a given return expectation (alternately, no additional expected return can be gained without increasing the risk of the portfolio). The Markowitz efficient portfolio is the set of all portfolios that will give the highest expected return for each given level of risk.

We all know that the more risk we take the higher the expected return. Index investors use index mutual funds to construct portfolios that meet certain levels of risk. For example a retired person living off of his portfolio must lower his risk so that he does not run out of money. He does this by reducing his exposure to equities and the value asset classes. Keeping your fixed income allocation to your age is a good rule of thumb. My portfolio is currently 83 % fixed income assets and immediate annuities and 17% equities. the equities do not contain any value stocks because this asset class runs in spurts – for a period of time they do well followed by a lean period. I have a rather large amount of money invested in foreign equities because I believe that the dollar will continue to depreciate over time.

It can be shown that slice and dice portfolios have in the past produced fantastic returns. Experts who have written good books on indexing have model portfolios that have done very well in good and bad times. Any book by Rick Ferri, Larry Sedro, and William Bernstein are recommended. It is a good idea to purchase and read all of the books by the above authors and the books by Jason Zweig that covers your brain and how it influences your portfolio decisions.

Slice and dice model portfolios can and do at times produce expected returns as high as 20% nominal above the market with 50% less risk than the market over 30 and 40 year periods. Achieving these fantastic returns depends on how the dice are rolled, random events that cannot be forecasted but are likely to occur several times over as long time spans.

Neuroeconomics

Neuroeconomics is a new discipline, the discussion of which warrants the following observations:

1. Cats can hear ultra sounds humans cannot.

2. When tabby jumps off your lap and heads for the kitchen she has heard some mice in the kitchen conversing with ultra sounds.

3. Humans see colors, your dog cannot.

4. Dogs can smell things at concentrations 1,000 times weaker than humans.

5. Bees can see infrared radiations. Humans cannot.

6. Blind people can identify their family and friends by their smell.

7. Young children's taste buds are 5 times more sensitive than their grandparents, and that is why your grandchildren do not like their choice of the food that they want them to eat. Don't worry, their selections will provide all the things they need to mature properly.

8. A small child needs loving handling from birth to develop properly.

9. Talk to your baby. They need to hear your voice from birth on, so their minds get wired to understand what you are saying and learn the language you speak.

10. If you are bilingual, use both languages at home. Your children will have no problem learning both languages simultaneously.

11. Every language has different speech sounds that must be learned at an early age to become familiar with the language at a young age to be fluent in the language. English has 41 different speech sounds while, Hawaiian only 12.

12. During the first few years of life, your children are establishing dedicated connections between their auditory receptors area in the auditory cortex. There are two speech centers in the brain one for speaking and the other for understanding what you hear.

Why do I make these observations? Because, in order to become a successful investor, you need to understand how your brain works. Each and every day, as an investor, your sensory system is bombarded with signals that may or may not be beneficial to your success as an investor if they are not properly evaluated by your limbic system an ancient part of your brain.

The anticipation of receiving a reward, say like your portfolio going up three days in a row will event triggers the same portion of your brain that a good shot of heroin satisfies a heroin addict. By way of example, most IPOs go up in value the first day and lose value after the 30 day period expires when the underwriter is permitted to manipulate the market to have a successful underwriting. Do those rascals know this? You bet they do. Then, they go down in price because of the difficulty of getting all that money working properly immediately.

As the CFO of a small OTC company, I took the opportunity to arrange a secondary offering of the company's stock. We needed some additional capital for new product development and our principal shareholder wanted to sell some of his unregistered stock as well. After going through all the traditional steps – like lunch at the Harvard club, listening to a shoe shine boy in the underwriter's office tout some stocks, we settled on a price at $8.50 per share, right where the market was selling our shares in the over-counter market.

As was customary, we flew to New York on a Monday several weeks later for the pricing meeting the following Tuesday. On the previous week, our stock took a bath, late Friday afternoon at about 30 minutes before closing. I rushed down to the market maker in Los Angeles for our stock (we were in the pink sheets at the time) to find out what was going on and I learned that there was a lot of shorting of our going on by customers of Wall Street firms.

This often happens to small OTC companies. Insiders were shorting our stock, knowing they will be covered by the offering if the price was busted or later after the 30 day distribution period was over. I had a little talk with the boss and told him what was happening – shall we fight or run? I said, "Harold, lets fight but let's make sure we win." We called some friends in Miami told them how many shares to buy and guaranteed them they would not lose money. Then, I told someone I knew who was with the Wall Street Journal and Barons, whom I suspected had just fewer than 5% of our stock.

At the Tuesday pricing meeting we had our fish or cut bait meeting. The lead underwriter wanted to price the offering at $7 a share. I wanted the $8.50 we had agreed to several weeks earlier. I suggested we go over who stood the most to lose if the offering did not go through and we decided to cancel the offering.

I then told them our situation. I wrote the S-1 red herring, our lawyer was to be paid with a 5,000 share option on the stock to sign off as the lawyer, and I had offered to buy his option in any case. Our auditor had made a mistake, failing to verify the post-closing entries in our books several years earlier and owed me an audited stub period. Harold wanted an excuse to visit his daughter, who lived in New York. And, I told them that we would go right home right now without suffering any losses unless we got our $8.50 a share. We won, got our price and the story made the rounds on the Street as good rumors have a way of doing. What happened was that the underwriter caved in because he had far more to lose than we did.

Later, as punishment, I refused to pay their attorney's fees for filing the blue sky laws on the basis that my secretary filled out all the forms in Los Angeles. I paid him $1000 for the phone call to satisfy Texas's questions. As further punishment, I called my new friend, the Barron's guy, and he unloaded his shares on the syndicate during the price stabilization period.

I returned to Wall Street a month or so later to give pep talk to the brokers, and a little speech on the company's future to help with distribution of the shares. It was then that I met

Charles Ellis. Charley asked me if I believed all that I was telling the brokers. I told him that this offering was as good as any other one. He asked for my card and several years later I received a complimentary copy of his book titled, The Loser's Game, and, after I read it, I immediately became an indexer.

Vanguard, the investor's friend

I would like to tell you about a friend of every investor whom you should know because it means money in your pocket. John Bogle graduated from Princeton in 1951, the same year I graduated from Claremont men's college. His senior thesis was tilled Mutual Funds can make no claims over Market Averages. Bogle wrote that his inspiration for starting an index fund came from three sources, all of which confirmed his 1951 research: Paul Samuelsson's paper Challenge to Judgment, Charles Ellis' 1975 study The Loser's Game and al Ehrbar's Fortune Magazine 1975 article on indexing.

Today, no Wall Street firm tries to make money indexing because they can't figure out how to make money selling index funds. Vanguard is a non-profit company owned by the shareholders of Vanguard Funds. Based on 2009 industry average expense ratios, actively managed mutual funds are 1.19% and Vanguard's expense ratio is only 0.23 percent – five times lower.

A 30 year-old investor with family earned income of $50,000 a year saving 12% and investing in index funds can build a portfolio, after 40 years, just on the difference in expenses alone, worth $2,666,555 versus just $290,900 for the average actively managed mutual fund with an identical portfolio.

My thesis was titled Personal Liberty and the Managed Economy, which forecasted the collapse of the Russian managed economy 40 years later. Socialism just cannot compete with free market economies in today's world markets. Actively managed mutual funds just cannot compete with index fund mutual funds.

Vanguard has a number of policies and schemes to prevent speculators from damaging the index funds by speculators. For example, for their index funds, they close trading two hours before the market closes thus preventing speculators from placing trades just before the market closes forcing vanguard to buy or sell shares in a fund the next trading day that may be at higher or lower prices.

Vanguard puts a gap between each equity asset class so that, as often happens, stock in one asset class bounces between say small and medium asset classes the fund does not have to trade until the stock makes up its mind so to speak. Sometimes speculators start to trade their index funds of follow a crowd chasing certain asset classes to their detriment of buy and hold investors so vanguard will add a fee to trade or just close the fund to new investors.

Make a plan of action

Write down some things that you know and from time to time read them to yourself, like:

-I know that I should buy low and hold my stocks until I retire and then sell high.

-I know that the market is usually right and that stocks are usually priced correctly.

-Is the market nervous or is it just me?

Look at the VIX, and if it is around 20, you are okay, but if it is climbing toward 50 or so, your portfolio is in for a rough ride, so get ready to save a little more and gather some funds because stocks are going on sale. Say to yourself, "I am not worried because it is normal for stocks to go on sale from time to time." Bear markets usually last for two or three years, while bull markets last much longer.

If you are relatively young, say in your twenties or thirties, or even a little older, you have 40 years to accumulate your nest egg, so look forward to accumulating your invested funds. Now get a notebook, crank up the computer and go to a web site like MoneyChimp to develop your plan. The web site is named after a contest in the WSJ, with a chimpanzee throwing darts at a page in the WSJ and some of Wall Street's best stock pickers. The monkey won. Now, go to the area where you can use the site to run some numbers. Enter the size of your portfolio, then the rate at which you think that your portfolio will grow somewhere between 7% and 9%. Then, enter the amount you plan to add to your portfolio each month. I recommend 12.5 to 15.5% of the family earned income. Then, the number of years the left for your accumulation phase.

Now you should have a look at any pension income and estimate your social security. For those of you with a good pension plan and accumulated social security, part of your problem is solved and you can take more risk so count on a very aggressive portfolio. For those of you who are risk adverse you too can have an aggressive portfolio. An aggressive portfolio has value stocks, an overload of small cap stocks and an asset allocation of 30% debt and 70% equities. A good ratio is to keep your debt at your age. It is a good idea to keep an eye on the VIX, which is a measure of the volatility of the market. Your allocation to foreign equities should be about 30% of your domestic. A good way to handle this allocation business is to place in your portfolio two very broad index funds. Vanguard's total domestic stock index fund and their total foreign stock index fund that has a nice allocation of small cap stocks.

The Future

History tells us and Gordon's equation tells us that these are good times to invest in equities. But you are cautioned not to get greedy. If your savings are such that you do not have to take risks, invest your funds in immediate annuities and fixed income short term bonds. You will find definitions of the above terms in the books of the authors I recommend.

Now here is my take on the Wall Street meltdown. Any time our government passes out guarantees, they are asking for problems. It happened in housing, in guaranteed pension plans, and bail out of those companies who take on too much risk. The minute the government legislates a guarantee there are many very smart people trying to figure out how to make tons of money from the situation.

FHA home loan guarantees are a prime example. The cost of insuring a loan was far less than the profit originating loans – think big return no risk. The requirement for a large down payment – simple solution – jack up the price by $20,000, and give the buyer the money for the down payment. You know it wasn't until mid-July 2009 that the FHA figured out how these buyers got their down payment.

Take Social Security. Since 1970, the system was in big trouble and Congress knew it and they did nothing to repair the damage. Knowing the birth rate and the death rate anyone can, with any brains, forecast the impending problem. But that is not how our government works. Politicians spent all the Social Security taxes that had been withheld. There is only one way to solve this problem – that is a Constitutional amendment to limit terms of Congressional members to two terms and prosecute those who use their power to make illegal money. That bunch in Washington is a smart bunch but they lack common sense. Their need to be re-elected overshadows what they should do. They know this and ignore the consequences.

Your stock portfolio grows just like a fetus. A baby puts on about one ounce by the end of the first trimester. Your stock portfolio gains about 13% of its final sum at the end of your accumulation phase at about the first five years. By the end of the second trimester, the baby weighs 9% of its final birth weight adds 27% of its final value. During the third trimester, the baby puts on 67% of its final birth weight while your portfolio will gain 60% of its total amount at retirement.

This is how buy and hold works and why it is so important to avoid excessive portfolio expenses and taxes caused by portfolio turnover and trading costs.

A study by William Bernstein showed that over a recent 29 year period (ending in 2009) that a total stock market portfolio returned 10.4% and that just 25% of the stocks made all the money while the other 75% lost about 2% for the period. Show me someone that can pick the 25% of the 8,600 common stock shares traded today over the next 40 years that will be in the group of winners. You bet it can't be done. A portfolio of index funds can produce these and even greater returns. In fact four a young couple saving 12% of their earned income can expect in the neighborhood of $2,500,000 after forty years with a slice and dice index fund portfolio with a probably of somewhere around 85% or by placing your funds with a full service broker you will be lucky to amass say $150,000 while the broker will have about five times that amount.

Remember

The premium for large cap value stocks in a slice and dice portfolio has in the past outperformed the market by 10% over a 20 year period and by 20% over a 35 year period. This does not mean that it will happen during your accumulation period no but the odds are in your favor. High returns require taking high risks. Your ability to take high risks depends on your age and the time available prior to retirement and most important what you have learned about the market.

It is highly unlikely that Medicare and social security benefits will be as generous in the past, so you should be careful with your money. Any who guarantees even reasonable returns is a scam artist.

Searching for bargains in the stock market is a loser's game. There are people who with skill and luck that have been able to outperform the market but no one has ever been able to identify them before the fact and only one person has even suggested how to identify them. Our most recent guru was Bill Miller who, after 15 years beating the market took a beating the next three years.

Over a recent 29 year period the domestic market returned 10.4%.and all this was done by 25% of the stocks, the other 75% lost 2%. The finical services industry charges outrageous fees for mediocre results. 50% of American workers have not even figured out how much they will need to retire. Those who have and are saving have an average of only about $25,000 saved. From 1984 to 2000 90% of investors' portfolios earned 5.23% while the market returned 16.2%.

Here is a bit of data to remember: A study of market timing recently came up with the following: for 2,000 trading days that's almost ten years. The market was up 357%. Miss the 10 best days and your return would have been 7.4%, miss the 50 best days and your return would have been zero zip. It is not possible to make reliable predictions when the market will rise or fall. If it were possible the market could not rise and fall the way it does. A retirement savings program requires at least 30 years to mature. In the first trimester you will have gained 13% of your goal. Over the next trimester another 27% and the final trimester 60%.

At about the age of 72, immediate annuities are a bargain. Those who die before the median age are helping you getting those high returns and paying for your golden years. One of my annuities purchased several years ago returns 12.7% for life. A good rule to follow is that if you consider that every stock broker, insurance salesman or investment advisor you are likely to meet as a common criminal you will survive the perils of the market. Hedge funds are gambling with your money and taking 2% for on average for losing your money and 20% of the profits if any.

Stock prices go up or down because of random events on cannot predict. In ancient Babylon contracts had to be notarized to be valid in court. The notary had to guarantee that the loan was for a capital project not for consumption. Don't expect the same guarantees from the stock market.

Best regards,

Gordon L. Eade

APPENDIXES

APPENDIX ONE INVESTING TIPS BY GORDON

Investing Tips by Gordon #1 Financial Intermediation

The sum total of all those advisory fees, market expenditure's, sales loads, brokerage commissions, custody and legal fees, and securities processing expenses add up to approximately $350,000,000,000 per year, or about 25% of the market return. Clearly, this massive drag on the profits that industry siphons off needs a careful look to see where we can cut costs. First, let's see where the money goes:

· Investment banks and brokers— $220 billion
· Direct mutual fund costs— $70 billion
· Pension fund management costs—$15 billion
· Personal financial advisors—$5 billion
· Hedge funds—$25 billion
· Annuities—$15 billion

Comparing the average active mutual fund with an index fund we find that we can save costs in the following areas: ·

Transaction costs: 30%—index funds seldom trade—active funds trade often.

Expenses: 30%—money spent on fund expenses is lost forever and has a negative compounding effect on funds available for retirement or other purposes.

Taxes: 67%—Uncle Sam's take is the largest of all.

Now let's examine the cumulative effect of this difference over one's investment. We are going to look at a couple saving 12% of their pretax income and investing in the average actively managed fund versus a broad market index fund over a 20year period. After taxes the average active fund accumulates the sum of $495,909 while the index fund accumulates $778,107, a difference of $282,198.

There is more bad news coming for the active investor. First, there is no known method to discovering a fund that will outperform a broad market index fund. Second, the odds are 3 to 4 that the fund you do select will underperform the index next year. Third, funds beating the index fund performance this year rarely beat the index the following year. If we look at longer periods of time, we see the magnitude of the problem. For the 14 years ending 2004, one single fund out of 10,000 mutual funds beat the performance of the S&P 500 index and then only by 1%. The fund was a "value fund" by Legg Mason managed by Bill Miller.

Investing Tips by Gordon #2 Retirement Planning

The only portions of the population who can count on their retirement benefits are those working for city, county, state, and federal governments. Even these entities currently face severe underfunding to the tune of $2,000,000,000, but they will get their pensions—you will pay for their good fortune. For those in the 40 to 45 age group, you can count on the full benefit retirement age being about 73 for social security benefits with reduced benefits pegged to your means to finance your own retirement. I don't want to debate the subject but to state simply, this is a reasonably accurate forecast by which to plan for the future. Any other scenario does not meet the test of a feasible solution.

This is going to be a very tough decision for those in politics, but it is a problem that has been known since 1960 when we started escalating social security contributions. Medical costs are a bigger problem, and the solution here will be a combination of tort reform—that is, limiting malpractice awards and placing the burden for sensible medical spending on the patient. By way of example, in my little town, an ambulance ride to the hospital a maximum of 7 miles costs $300 and emergency room treatment another $300 for a nose bleed.

If you and your spouse want to live a comfortable retirement life, you must do two things. First, you must save a minimum of 12% of your gross income, have your home paid for by your retirement date, and be debt free. Second, you must learn how to manage your own portfolio of stocks and bonds using index funds. The hardest task awaiting you is to overcome the fear and greed present in owning marketable securities—greed that will cause you to make foolish and disastrous decisions and fear you will experience when the market declines 20% or 30% for several years as it has and will do so again at some time in the future. I guarantee. When the market takes a dive, think of this: stocks are on sale – better buy some now before they go up.

Investing Tips by Gordon #3 Vanguard Diehards

There is a group of individual investors who follow what is known as passive investing techniques—that is, they use index funds. These investors practice methods used by some of the largest pension plans and trusts. Diehards use index funds to form portfolios of stocks and bonds that obtain superior returns at reduced risk. They follow methods set down by some of the finest minds in the academic community when it comes to investing in marketable securities. Diehards use index funds managed by the Vanguard Group, a unique organization in the financial services industry, in that investors are charged only the cost of running Vanguard funds. To contact Vanguard, go to their website at www.vanguard.com[1]. Diehards use a forum sponsored by Morning Star (www.MorningStar.com), a provider of data on mutual funds. This forum has, since its inception, hosted some 350,000 conversations on approximately 40,000 topics. The form receives some 25,000 hits daily. Once at the website, go to Discuss, then Diehards. The group has an annual get together where some 100 Diehards meet to discuss their investments. Recently, local chapters have been formed where individual investors meet on an informal basis. Any investor with a question or problem can post his question on the Diehard forum and receive advice and counsel from the many "experts" who monitor the website.

---

1.   http://www.vanguard.com

Investing Tips by Gordon #4 Huge Dividend Payers

Retirees need an inflation protected income stream and dividend paying stocks fit the bill. Recent tax changes have become favorable to encourage increasing dividend payouts. Companies that increase their dividends also provide inflation protection even during high periods of inflation. Dividend paying stocks of the S&P 500 index have outperformed non-dividend payers by $514,132 to $374,912 since 1975 on a $10k lump sum investment. The new 15% dividend tax rate certainly helps attract investors to dividend paying stocks. Today, a retired married couple, using income from investments for living expenses, can earn $59K annually (after personal exemption and standard deduction) in qualified dividends from a taxable account and pay just 5% tax to the federal government. On a practical level, I tend to agree with William Bernstein who stated in an Efficient Frontier article that he would rather have the corporation pay out dividends and borrow for their new projects compared to using retained earnings. His feeling, and my corporate experience concurs, that businesses are more conservative with their investments when they are financed as opposed to using internally generated funds. One way to assemble a portfolio of dividend paying stocks is to buy an Exchange Traded Fund called Dow Jones Select Dividend Index Fund (DVY). The index is composed of one hundred of the highest dividend yielding securities (excluding REITs) in the Dow Jones U.S. Total Stock Market Index, a broad based index representative of the total market for U.S. equity securities. To obtain current and price information go to www.ishares.com and use the password "ishares." Keep your eyes peeled for new Exchange Traded Funds that capture high dividend payers. I expect that many new ETFs will appear soon. For those interested in income securities see the new book by Ben Stein titled Yes, You Can Become a Successful Income Investor.

Investing Tips by Gordon #5 Modern Portfolio Theory

The cost savings of a tax efficient, low-cost index fund compounds at an exponential rate over time to produce awesome portfolio returns. The effect of dollar cost averaging and combining index funds, according to the Markowitz equations, add further to returns due to the bonus achieved from combining asset classes with low correlation coefficients. When tax management is performed during the regular annual portfolio rebalancing back to the selected asset allocation additional profits will accrue to the portfolio. Using these techniques, can easily double your portfolio return over a long period of time with considerably less risk compared to an actively managed mutual fund promoted by a broker. A series of model portfolios have been constructed for the investor who desires to achieve superior investment performance for his retirement. These portfolios have been constructed in accordance with Modern Portfolio Theory. Several automatic portfolios are also included where all these tax efficiencies and rebalancing tasks are performed for you at no additional cost. These portfolios are included in the appendix of my first book, How to Make Money in the Stock Market – Buy 2,500 Different Stocks – Pay No Commission. Think of this little book as a compilation of recipes for the investor who wants to achieve superior results at a level of risk below that associated with either active mutual funds or a portfolio selected by your broker. The author has compiled a suggested reading list for the do-it-yourself investor and a list of websites for you to use to check your selection with your peers with far more experience than you possess.

Investing Tips by Gordon #6 Actively Managed Mutual Funds

The majority of investors are sold actively managed funds by their investment advisor or by a stock broker. There are about 10,000 mutual funds today. Why so many? Well, they are extremely profitable for the fund sponsors and their employees. Academia and their students have been studying funds for many years and have arrived at the following conclusions: 1) Funds with a front-end load do not return profits higher than no load funds; 2) About 25% of mutual funds will outperform the market in any one year the ones that outperform by one percent or more do not outperform the following year. There is no method of selecting beforehand next years' funds that will outperform the market.

Fund managers are gambling with your money, attempting to earn large bonuses. · If you want to gamble, buy the latest hot fund. The average actively managed fund before expenses will perform exactly the same as the passively managed index fund. Since passively managed funds have much lower costs and expenses they will outperform over time all actively managed funds.

Excessive turnover creates taxable events, and the money lost to taxes is compounding to build your retirement portfolio. There have been fund managers who have outperformed the market in the past. There is no known method to find these geniuses beforehand. Their performance could have been just sheer chance. Out of 10,000 funds, only one has outperformed the market over the last 14 years. His name is Bill Miller and the fund is the Legg Mason Value Trust. In 2006 his, winning streak ended. If you feel lucky, go buy the fund, and let me know how you make out. More about actively managed and passively managed funds in further tips.

Investing Tips by Gordon #7 Roth IRAs

You are eligible to make a regular contribution to a Roth IRA even if you participate in a retirement plan maintained by your employer. These contributions can be as much as $5,500 or $6,500 for 2015. There are just two requirements. First, you or your spouse must have compensation or alimony income equal to the amount contributed. And second, your modified adjusted gross income can't exceed certain limits. The amount you can contribute is reduced gradually and then completely eliminated when your modified adjusted gross income exceeds a certain level. Make a rollover to a Roth IRA if: (a) your modified adjusted gross income is $100,000 or less, and (b) you're single or file jointly with your spouse. You'll have to pay tax in the year of the conversion, but for many people, the long-term savings outweigh the conversion tax. Distributions from Roth IRAs are tax-free until you've withdrawn all your regular contributions. After that, you'll withdraw your rollover (conversion) contributions, if any. Special rules apply when you withdraw your rollover contributions. When you've withdrawn all your contributions (regular and rollover), any subsequent withdrawals come from earnings. The withdrawals are tax-free if you're over age 59½ and at least five years have expired since you established your Roth IRA. Otherwise (with limited exceptions), they're taxable and potentially subject to the early withdrawal penalty. Credit to the website listed below. Like everything the government does the Roth rules are tricky—for a complete review see: http://www.fairmark.com/rothira/thumb.htm.

Investing Tips by Gordon #8 Financial Euphoria

Financial euphoria occurs when the market goes completely made and bids up the prices of securities beyond reasonable limits. The first documented episode occurred in the seventeenth century and is referred to as "Tulip Mania." Speculation became rampant, and one single tulip bulb was valued at $50,000.

Here is how these rare occurrences begin. A new artifact or development appears, and the price goes up. The increase attracts new buyers, and yet more buyers appear and the speculation goes on. There are those who are convinced that some new price enhancing circumstance has taken hold of the market. And there are those who are in the market simply to ride the price spiral up, knowing that madness has taken hold, and plan to get out at the last possible moment. There are those who warn of the coming episode but they are not welcome and are said to be motivated by either deficient understanding or uncontrolled envy of the process of enrichment. Those involved with the speculation are experiencing an increase in wealth. No one wishes to believe that this is fortuitous or undeserved; all wish to think that it's the result of their own superior insight or intuition. What happens next is that some event triggers a panic. Those who had been riding the price increases get out. Those who thought it would go on forever find their illusion destroyed. The speculative episode ends with a bang. And it repeats itself again 20 years or so later in some new form.

The most severe case occurred here in the U.S from 1999 to 2000 during the dot com craze when companies with no sales or earnings were bid up beyond reason. Many millions of dollars were lost by speculators and those who became convinced that price appreciation would continue forever.

Investing Tips by Gordon #9 Cost and return comparisons

Compare results over a 30 year period looking forward. Why 30 years? Well, a 43 year-old will go on full social security benefits at age 73 (an estimate by those studying future SS benefits). We will be comparing the average mutual fund with an index mutual fund—I am going to compare the costs and returns for an aggressively managed mutual fund and a passively managed index fund.

Aggressively managed mutual funds study and analyses securities in the pursuit of gains that exceed the market return while an index fund seeks to match the market. We are going to compare specifically the Vanguard Total Stock Market Index Fund, an exchange traded fund symbol (VTI). This fund is extremely tax efficient due to the fact that it contains in excess of 3,800 securities and trading is seldom required to match the index whereas the average mutual fund attempts to outperform and on average turns over its portfolio every 15 months incurring trading costs and capital gains distributions for its shareholders. The costs and profits for management of the actively managed mutual exceeds that of the above mentioned index fund by a factor of (1.5% to .07%) 21 times. All of these costs and expenses reduce the return on the portfolio each and every year for the 30 year period under examination. In fact, they reduce proceeds each and every year on a compounding basis. The average investor is not aware of the magnitude of the reduction in end portfolio value—your retirement nest egg. Buy just one fund and here are the results after 30 years:

After 30 years	Average Actively Managed Fund	Total Market Index Fund (VTI)
Total Return	$1,006,266	$1,006,266
Transaction Costs	$163,031	$39,231
Expense Ratio	$244,546	$18,308
Income Taxes	$309,759	$73,231
Total Cost	$717,336	$130,770
Net Return	$288,930	$875,496

It's the high portfolio turnover that kills the profitability of actively managed mutual funds that causes the increased transaction costs. It's the cost of security analysis and management that kills the return, and the taxes paid on capital gains that reduce the total return on a compounding basis. It is a fact that only 25% of all aggressively managed funds before taxes beat the index.

Investing Tips by Gordon #10 The Five Enemies You Must
Avoid

There are five traps awaiting the unwary investor:

· Actively managed mutual funds and the brokers that sell
them

· The media including financial newspapers and magazines,
newsletters, radio, and TV.

· Inflation

· Capital gains taxes

· The person you see in the mirror

Now, let's take these enemies one at a time and see what
you can do about them. You must simply avoid the brokers employed by full service brokerage firms. Simply stated, there is no
financial product sold by these very nice people that should be
in your stock or bond portfolio. I can assure you that you are no
match for these highly trained salesmen. You have no business
meeting them in person or talking with them on the phone.
They are in the business of transferring your money from your
pocket into theirs and are extremely skilled at it.

Free investment seminars are one place where you will
meet these folks. Their presentations include a speech by the
broker followed by a presentation by the mutual fund salesman. Here is how the scam works. A fund organizer starts 20
or so mutual funds. Each of these funds makes different bets
on the direction of three years or so, they merge the unsuccess-
ful funds into the best performer. The lousy fund's poor record
then disappears. Is this legal? You bet it is. When you look up
a fund's prior performance record in Lipper Analytics you will

note that when compared with the prior years' various sectors of the market with different weights of individual securities. After report, the fund will advance in its ranking. This is because under performing fund are either liquidated or merged into successful funds. We call this survivor bias and it has been estimated to average about 1.5%. Simply stated, fund data overstate the average performance of all mutual funds' returns by 1.5%. The second enemy may be found in the next article.

Investing Tips by Gordon #11 The media (including financial
   newspapers and magazines, newsletters, radio, and TV)

With very few exceptions, there is nothing in the media
that you need to know to manage your portfolio. There is, however, a columnist who writes a regular column you should read
in the Wall Street Journal. His name is Jonathan Clements. His
weekly column and archived past columns are available online
at the following website:

http://online.wsj.com/public/page/0,,sundayjournal_in-
dex.html.

Look for the search box and put in: "Jonathan Clements"
to see his past articles. Mr. Clements is an index fund enthu-
siast and recommends index funds for the individual investor
over all other strategies and has many fine suggestions for the
investor. The stuff you find in most other magazines and hear
on the radio or TV is worthless financial pornography. It has
been known for years that investment newsletters do not provide useful information for the investor. You are cautioned not
to subscribe to these publications unless you intend to lose
money. When you are surfing the web for financial information
and ideas, you are certain to draw attention to yourself, and
you will become the target of sales people willing to sell you
schemes to increase your profits in investing. Hardly a week
goes by that I do not receive solicitations of this type.

Recently, I received a call from a young man offering a computer program to select winning stocks. I am certain that he
was sincere and truly believed in the program he was offering for only $3,000 (regularly priced at $6,000.) The program
screened the history of 1,500 stocks on several hundred characteristics over the past 10 years and found the few that had extra-

ordinary profits for the lucky investor. Any statistician can tell you that it is always possible to find in a history of data the few stocks that have outperformed all others. Unfortunately, this tells us nothing about the future.

Investing Tips by Gordon #12 Inflation

Inflation is built into our monetary system and has averaged 3.5% for as long as the Federal Reserve has managed the economy. I graduated from college in 1951. The dollar earned in that year is worth 13 cents today. Some investors believe that one can partially protect against inflation by adding foreign securities to your portfolio. I subscribe to this camp. I believe that, by investing in the stock of European Common Market countries, one can hedge against inflation of the dollar. My reasoning is the controls that the common market countries must follow offer protection against inflation of the Euro. A security that allows one to invest in these countries is the Exchange Traded Fund called the Morgan Stanley Capital International (MSCI) European Market Union (EMU) Fund (symbol EZU). You buy this fund through a discount broker – a good one is Brown Co. – find them on the Internet. Another good way to mitigate some of the damage by inflation is to purchase TIPS Treasury Inflation Protection bonds. Vanguard has a fund that contains these securities for the individual investor.

Investing Tips by Gordon #13 The Worst Enemy

The markets are open for trading and some five billion shares will trade today. Ninety percent of all trades will occur on the orders of professional traders; that is, the managers of pension funds, mutual funds, hedge funds, and trusts. The balance of ten percent will be transactions of individual investors investing for their own accounts. Exactly 50% of trades will by parties who believe the stocks they buy are underpriced and the other 50% are by parties who think the stocks are overpriced.

Your worst enemy is looking right at you every morning in your mirror. Study after study has confirmed this indisputable fact. Every investor has to decide between a proven investing strategy backed by academic studies and data and hundreds of unproven ones marketed and sold by Wall Street.

The majority of Wall Street hype centers on timing the market and recommending undervalued securities or hot mutual funds. There is at least one piece of historical data that should convince skeptics that trying to "time the market" is most likely an exercise in futility. Out of the 936 months covering the period 1926 to 1933, the returns for the best 66 months (7%) averaged over 11%. The returns for the remaining 870 months (93%) averaged less than 0.02 percent per month. Trying to time investment decisions doesn't work because most of the action occurs over such brief, and unexpected, periods. So now we have established that a buy and hold strategy is best. What, then, should we buy and hold? The answer is to buy an index fund. For those who are taking title in a tax deferred account you have a broad choice of funds available.

However, for those of you who are taking title in a taxable account, buy a tax managed fund or a total market fund that tracks the entire stock market. The reason for that is that you want to minimize transactions. Academics have found that low turnover small investors actually beat the market before trading costs and high turnover investors underperform before costs. After costs of course underperformance was greater among high turnover investors. Evidence shows that the stocks people sell tend to outperform the stocks they hold. All this boils down to one simple rule: Buy an index fund and let it grow. Do not trade.

Investing Tips by Gordon #14 The Market

The markets are open for trading and some five billion shares will trade today. Ninety percent of all trades will occur on the orders of professional traders; that is, the managers of pension funds, mutual funds, hedge funds, and trusts. The balance of ten percent will be transactions of individual investors investing for their own accounts. Exactly 50% of trades will by parties who believe the stocks they buy are underpriced and the other 50% are by parties who think the stocks are overpriced.

During the trading day, prices will move according to the supply and demand of the respective parties. The publication of new developments and news of specific companies is immediately incorporated into stock prices of individual companies and their sector. It is believed that prices migrate to the point to facilitate a trade and, in response to new information on specific issues, market sectors and the markets general, the opinion of the economy and foreign trade.

Investing Tips #15 Is the stock market a sum zero game?

First, investing is not a zero sum game. In fact it is a winner's game – defined as a game in which everyone playing can win. They just simply have to accept market returns and they will earn the equity risk premium.

Second, beating the market is a zero sum game before expenses, but a negative sum game after expenses. That makes it a loser's game in the aggregate. A loser's game is one where the odds of winning are so poor it doesn't pay to try to win. The way to win a loser's game is to not play. In this case, not playing means accepting market returns.

Investing Tips #16 Understanding Risk

A typical actively managed mutual fund or a portfolio of stocks recommended by a full service broker has about 30% more risk than the market. Investors are risk adverse, which means they demand additional returns over and above the market return to hold the more risky securities. Please understand that the only way to beat market returns is to select those stocks that will over perform the market.

When you adopt this strategy your portfolio will contain uncompensated risk – that is risk for which there is no concomitant return. Unless you are lucky, such a strategy leads to an underperforming portfolio. We have a very good but not perfect method of ranking stocks and bonds by their risk characteristics. It is simply a statistically measure of the securities volatility or how much its market price varies over time. More risky securities will exhibit higher volatility while less risky securities will have lower volatility.

In 1953 a young college student named Harry Markowitz selected a statistical measure of volatility, called the standard deviation, to represent risk and coupled this expression to the securities average price. For the first time, Wall Street had a measure of risk. Further, Harry discovered that selecting securities whose prices did not move in tandem with changes in the economy could lower the risk of a portfolio of stocks. In fact, Harry showed by means of a mathematical formula that on could construct a portfolio that would obtain the highest return for any level of risk. We call this method Modern Portfolio Theory (MPT).

Let me draw for you a parallel example that occurs in your wife's kitchen every day. Let's say she has decided to make you some cookies. Take flour, butter, sugar, and a pinch of salt, mix and add some chocolate chips in the correct quantities, pop the mixture into a 325 degree oven for 15 minutes and a new product appears- the chocolate chip cookie. It has neither the appearance, texture nor flavor of any of its component parts. Well, portfolios work in the same way. Our components are asset classes of equities such as large and small cap stocks, growth and value stocks and fixed income securities and the quantities of each for various levels of risks are recipes called model portfolios. In my book I show the investor a number of model portfolios designed using the principles of modern portfolio theory to capture the small-cap and value premiums.

You do not need to know how these portfolios are constructed to use them, nor does your wife need to be a food chemist to use and follow the recipes to obtain good results.

Investing Tips #17 Quotations from investing experts

"A low-cost index fund is the most sensible equity investment for the great majority of investors. My mentor, Ben Graham, took this position many years ago, and everything I have seen since convinces me of its truth." Warren Buffet

"Of the 355 equity funds in 1970, fully 233 of those funds have gone out of business. Only 24 outpaced the market by more than 1% a year. These are terrible odds." Jack Bogle

"Most investors would be better off in an index fund." Peter Lynch

"Only about one out of every four equity funds outperforms the stock market. That's why I'm a firm believer in the power of indexing." Charles Schwab
"Index funds are perhaps the most underrated stock funds in existence." Mutual Funds for Dummies

"The fund industry's dirty little secret: most actively managed funds never do as well as their benchmark." Arthur Levitt, Former
Chairman, SEC

"Over the long-term, the superiority of indexing is a mathematical certainty." Jason Zweig, senior writer for Money Magazine

"The media focuses on the temporarily winning active funds that score the more spectacular bull's eyes, not index funds that score every year and accumulate less flashy, but ultimately winning, scores." W. Scott Simon, author

"I love index funds." William Sharpe, Nobel Laureate

"Indexing is for winners only." Jane Bryant Quinn, author, syndicated columnist

"Most people should simply have index funds so they can keep their fees low and their taxes down." Jack Meyer, CEO, Harvard Management

"Four years ago I was a fan of index funds. Today I am a true believer." Jonathan Clements, senior writer, Wall Street Journal

"We find that on average, active management reduces a portfolio's returns and increases its volatility compared with a static index." Vanguard Investment Counseling & Research Analysis

"They're just not going to do it (beat the market). It's just not going to happen. Daniel Kahneman, Nobel Laureate

"I was not always an obnoxious indexing zealot. Ten years of believing in and selling active management strategies in the brokerage industry made me this way." Rick Ferri, CFA, author

"Active portfolio management thus tends to generate lower returns and higher taxes." John Haslem, author

"Indexing virtually guarantees you superior performance." Bill Bernstein, author, financial adviser

"Index funds save on management and marketing expenses, reduce transaction costs, defer capital gain, and control risk—and in the process beat the vast majority of actively managed mutual funds." Good & Hermansen, authors

"In every asset class where they are available. Index! Four of five funds will fail to meet or beat an appropriate index." Frank Armstrong, author, financial adviser

"With an index fund—the certainty of keeping up with the market is a very worthwhile trade-off for the possibility of beating it." Jack Brennan, CEO Vanguard

"Searching through a list of 234 domestic equity funds that have survived for 20 years, only 31 did better than the Vanguard 500 Index. That means the odds are really, really poor that any of us will do better than a low-cost broad index fund." Scott Burns, syndicated columnist

"Index funds offer much more than superior returns. They also provide maximum diversification, no overlap, no style drift, no manager changes, lower turnover, lower expenses, lower taxes, greater simplicity and peace of mind." Taylor Larimore, author

"Choosing actively managed funds is the triumph of hope over reason and experience." Larry Swedroe, author, financial adviser

"It's just not true that you can't beat the market. Every year about one-third do it. Of course, each year it is a different group." Robert Stovall, investment manager

"Giving up the futile pursuit of beating the market is the surest way to increase your investment efficiency and enhance your financial peace of mind." Ron Ross, author and adviser

"It is basically impossible to beat the market." Prof. Eugene Fama

"Indexing is a marvelous technique. I wasn't a true believer, I was just an ignoramus. Now I am a convert. Indexing is an extraordinarily sophisticated thing to do." Douglas Dial, former CREF portfolio manager

"Simple buy-and-hold index investing is one of the best, most efficient ways to grow your money. Michael Lebouf, Ph.D., author

"The best plan for most of us, is to commit to buying some index funds and do nothing else." Charles Ellis, author

"With the market beating 91% of surviving managers since the beginning of 1982, it looks pretty efficient to me." Bill Miller, portfolio manager

"We should just forget about choosing fund managers and settle for index funds to mimic the market." Pat Regnier, former Morningstar analyst

"Because active and passive returns are equal before cost, and because active managers bear greater cost, it follows that the after-cost return from active management MUST be lower than that from passive management." Wm Sharpe, Nobel Laureate

"The most efficient way to diversify a stock portfolio is with a low fee index fund." Paul Samuelson, Nobel Laureate

"We find that on average, active management reduces a portfolio's returns and increases its volatility compared with a static index implementation of the portfolio's asset allocation policy." Vanguard study

"Buy and hold. Diversify. Put your money in Index Funds." Justin Fox, Fortune senior writer

"Index funds save on management and marketing expenses, reduce transaction costs, defer capital-gain, and control risk—and in the process, beat the vast majority of actively man-age mutual funds." Good & Hermansen, authors

"You should switch all your investment in stocks to index funds as soon as possible, after giving proper consideration to any tax consequences." Chandan Sengupta, author

"I am somewhat skeptical about anyone's ability to consistently beat the market." Moshe Milevsky, author

"With an index fund—the certainty of keeping up with the market is a very worthwhile trade-off for the possibility of beat-ing it." Jack Brennan, Vanguard CEO

"With a very simple and basic understanding of index funds, you can consistently beat 70% to 80% of all professionally managed index funds." Tweddell & Pierce, authors

"Invest in a stock index mutual fund. What a brilliant, inge-nious, common sense idea that I can't take credit for, but can re-ligiously pass along to those of you who want to unclutter your

financial lives and own a sophisticated portfolio." Bill Schulthe-
is, author

"For most of us, trying to beat the market leads to disastrous results." Prof. Jeremy Siegel, author

"The surest way to make money in the stock market is not to
work very hard at it. Don't try to outsmart the market; settle
for matching it. Put most of your money in an index mutual
fund." Gary Belsky, author

"My strongest commitment in the mutual fund arena is to index funds." Richard Young, editor

"I recommend that the long-term buy-and-hold portion of
your equity portfolio be invested in equity mutual funds." Shel-
don Jacobs, author

"The smartest thing people can do if they want money in the
equities market is buy an index fund that is run for 30 basis
points a year and forget about it." Elliot Spitzer, NY Attorney
General

"The only consistent superior performer is the market itself and the only way to capture the superior consistency is to invest in a properly diversified portfolio of index funds." Rex Sinquefield, researcher

"It's extremely difficult to beat the market." Peter Brimlow, Forbes senior editor

"There can be no question that indexing for most categories of taxable investor and for most marketable conditions, will outperform conventional active management." Robert Arnott, CEO First Quadrant

"A passive index fund managed by a not-for-profit investment management organization represents the combination most likely to satisfy investor aspirations." David Swensen, author

"The S&P index benchmarks outperformed their active peer funds in all nine Morningstar style boxes over the past ten years." Gus Sauter, Vanguard

"It's amazing to me that, by one estimate, only 14% of money is indexed in this country!! What a shame." Lynn O'Shaughnessy, author

"I continue to believe that unless you are extremely skilled (and lucky) for most investors, index funds remain the simplest and most efficient vehicle for investing in stocks." Annette Thou, author

"When you realize how few advisors have beaten the market over the last several decades, you may acquire the discipline to do something even better: become a long-term index fund investor." Mark Hulbert, newsletter tracker

"If it weren't for noise, 98% of investors would see what's going on and buy passive strategies." Kenneth R French

"Scholarly work by Burton Malkiel, Eugene Fama and others has proved that it is the rare investor who can outperform the overall market." Ben Stein, NY Times

"Choosing actively managed funds is the triumph of hope over reason and experience." Larry Swedroe, author

"Indexing virtually guarantees you superior performance." Bill Bernstein, author

"Indexing is an extraordinarily sophisticated thing to do." Douglas Dial, CREF

"With the market beating 91% of surviving managers since the beginning of 1982, it looks pretty efficient to me." Bill Miller, portfolio manager

"Buy and hold. Diversify. Put your money in Index Funds." Justin Fox, Fortune senior writer

"For most of us, trying to beat the market leads to disastrous results." Prof. Jeremy Siegel, author

"A passive index fund managed by a not-for-profit investment management organization represents the combination most likely to satisfy investor aspirations." David Swensen, author and Yale portfolio manager

"Most people should simply have index funds so they can keep their fees low and their taxes down. No doubt about it." Jack Meyer, Harvard portfolio manager

"Beating an index is no piece of cake anywhere in the style box." Russel Kinnel, Morningstar Director of Fund Research

"Index funds. They aren't perfect, but they are better than all the other forms that have been tried." Scott Burns, syndicated columnist

"Just 19 percent of U.S. mutual funds that have existed since mid-1980 were able to beat the S&P 500 through May of 2006" Lipper

"Most investors should simply invest in index funds." Robert Rubin, Former Secretary of the Treasury

APPENDIX TWO LONGEVITY

Census data shows us that we people America are living longer. A couple in their mid-seventies have a good chance that of one of them living to their living to their mid- nineties. This is extremely important and affects your entire investment plan. First, you can be sure that social security will not kick in until the age of seventy five so your accumulation period, defined the time between the ages of 30 until 75, is approximately 45 years. As a consequence you have 45 years for your portfolio to grow. We call these 45 years the accumulation period. Here is a list of the things you should consider:

- The longer the accumulation period (the period you have earned income from labor) the bigger your retirement investment will become. But the longer the accumulation period, the more money you will need to counter inflation (count on 3% increase per year.)

- Having your investment funds in a tax free account becomes vital. (see Roth IRA's)

- Keep stock trading that will trigger taxable events to a minimum.

- At the age of 75 consider purchasing an immediate annuity from an AAA rated insurance company".

APPENDIX THREE ABOUT BROKERS

- Brokers take a simple examination consisting of questions about what a broker can and cannot say when talking with a client.

- There are no educational requirements compared with the requirement for education and skill for a barber in your state.

- He will sell you actively managed mutual funds. The front-end load is money that the mutual fund pays him.

- The broker will sell you those stocks that earn him the highest commission..

- He has no fiduciary duty to sell you the product with the lowest cost or if he knows an index fund.

- The majority of investors buy actively managed funds suggested by their broker.

- These funds will have front end loads and 10b1 fees

- He will tout the fund's 1,3, and 5 year average annual return

- Never will the broker mention a measure of the risk of the investment

•Actively managed mutual funds have one-third risk more than the market index fund.

•The fund he sells you has been selected by evaluating the fund's tract record, studies show that this is not an accurate method of selecting a fund that will meet or beat the market return.

•In fact there is no known method of selecting a fund that will outperform the market.

•Actively managed have a portfolio turnover of 80% to 100% per year triggering taxable events, that according to studies can reduce the funds after tax earnings by 1% to 2.5% per year.

•Can a stock Broker earn a living by selling you the proper securities for your age and risk tolerance? No it is doubtful that he can.

•But he is very skillful at transferring money from your bank account to his.

•Brokers are trained to sell stocks and extra high commissions are earned when he unloads toxic merchandise setting in the firm's inventory.

•It's not only stocks that are peddled this way but bonds as well.

APPENDIX FOUR SELLING SCRIPTS

From an unknown source

Sometimes in the course of preparing our cases we have been able to obtain "sales scripts" which stockbrokers have used to push worthless stock on unsuspecting investors. "Sales scripts" are written by individual stockbrokers, a stock promoter or management and given to stockbrokers to help those open accounts and sell stock. These sales scripts were used at a brokerage firm that has since gone out of business in part due to regulatory pressures and law suits from investors who were defrauded by the firm's fraudulent practices and illegal manipulation of small stocks.

If you ever receive a call from someone like this hang up the phone or contact your state securities commissioner.

Sales Script #1:

> Mr. Burns, We've been on the phone for 10 minutes now and you sound like a hell of a nice guy. Let me ask you a question. Why is it that 90% of the people who invest in the market lose money or see mediocre results? Why do the Warren Buffets, the Carl Icahns – why are they always the ones who seem to make the money?

> I'll tell you why. It's because they deal with the right people who are very well connected. Believe me. I am one of those people. I have connections all over the street. You name the firm and BELIEVE ME, I know someone there.

I know how you feel. I am a couple thousand miles away, you don't know me, and we've never done business together. I can appreciate that. Perhaps you've lost money in the past with other brokers, and you're annoyed, and you know what, I'm a little annoyed too because it makes my job 10 times harder than it has to be.

Mr. Burns, if you work with me on 1,000 shares of Buskins Buckets you will be doing so much more than buying a small piece of a phenomenal company. You'll be buying a broker who really cares about his clients. BELEVE ME, I am at my office every day at 7:30 in the morning breaking my ass to make money for my clients. I don't leave until 10 at night this business means everything to me.

Do this. Go with me on 1,000 shares.

Sales Script #2

Mr. Burns, I deal with the most sophisticated investors, presidents and CEO's of major public corporations from Maine to California.

Over the next twelve months you are going to realize this was the best call you've ever gotten from a broker. You're going to thank me for giving you the little push you need today. Give me the shot, and you'll be very, impressed.

Go with 200 shares.

Sales Script #3

I'm about to tell you something that nobody on Wall Street will ever tell you, my commission on 1 share or 10,000 shares is $75. I split that with the firm and the government.

APPENDIX FIVE MARKET TIMING

Market timing: Trinity Investment Management Corporation, Boston, Massachusetts, October 1994, states that the minimum batting averages necessary for a market timer to outperform a continuously and fully invested indexer. In order to achieve this, a market timer would have to have a minimum forecasting accuracy of at least 80% for rising markets and 90% for falling markets. In effect , a market timer would be required to bat about .700 to beat an indexer fully invested in the market at all timing.

APPENDIX SIX ABOUT THE VALUE PREMIUM

Value stocks are defined as stocks with a low book to price ration. Rick Ferri speaks about the value premium. I believe, as he does, that the value premium in behavioral, but only to the extent that people expect a higher return for taking more perceived risk. Prices are a reflection of perceived risk. Even if that perception is proved to be incorrect over time, people will act today based on whatever information is available. That is how the market prices securities. And when prices are falling like a rock, there is a lot more perceived risk than there might be over the long-term. Fannie Mae and Freddie Mac are good examples. The long-term risk of Fannie and Freddie going out of business is remote, but there is a real possibility that short-term investors will lose a lot of money fast. The price of those securities must fall to reflect both fundamental risk and short-term trading risk.

APPENDIX SEVEN LONG TERM RETURNS

Long-Term Returns of NYSE/AMEX/NASDAQ Stocks Ranked by Size,
1926-2000

Size (deciles)	Compound Return	Annual Risk	Beta	Largest firm in deciles	Total capitalization
Largest	10.26%	19.0%	0.91	$524.35 B	$11,757 B
2	11.32%	22.7%	1.04	$10.34 B	$1,797 B
3	10.59%	24.5%	1.09	$4.14 B	$865 B
4	11.52%	27.6%	1.13	$2.18 B	$547 B
5	11.32%	30.1%	1.16	$1.33 B	$400 B
6	11.31%	30.2%	1.18	$840.0 M	$287 B
7	10.99%	32.5%	1.24	$537.7 M	$222 B
8	11.27%	34.7%	1.28	$333.4 M	$138 B
9	12.59%	38.8%	1.34	$192.6 M	$117 B
Smallest	16.71%	49.3%	1.42	$84.5 M	$74 B

*Investors are cautioned not to use these data to plan their returns when saving for retirement. You are advised to use Gordon's Equation to forecast future returns. Further it is a better idea to use the equation to forecast the returns for each asset class in your portfolio. Gordon's equation at present indicates a real return of from 6% to 8% for equities and 2% for bonds. A conservative number for inflation for the foreseeable future would be 3%.

APPENDIX EIGHT HISTORY OF ACTIVELY MANAGED PORTFOLIOS

Active investment managers attempt to select superior securities or time markets to earn results that consistently outperform a static benchmark. You would think, based on the marketing messages from active managers, that they have been successful at delivering robust returns over the decades. This isn't the case. In fact, active managers as a group have consistently underperformed their benchmarks for almost a century.

Alfred C. Cowles, III was the first person to quantify the results of active management in the early 1930s. Cowles meticulously measured the performance of professional stock forecasters and market timers over a period ending in June 1932. Shortly thereafter, he published his findings in an article titled *Can Stock Market Forecasters Forecast*? Cowles's conclusion was simple and direct, "It is doubtful."

Cowles divided active management into two strategies: security selection and market timing. He then attempted to measure the presence of each skill separately.

Using two separate sets of data from insurance company returns and securities analysts' picks, Cowles found that only about 1 in 3 were able to select stocks that outperformed the general market over a period of about 5 years. In addition, he measured the securities analyst performance to be about 1.4 percent annually below the market, and the insurance companies performed by about 4.7 percent below the market. The insurance companies had real investment costs while the analysts' results were only hypothetical. This may have accounted for the large difference in underperformance.

Cowles also noted that the winning analysts and insurance funds may have a tough time proving they had skill because their results were worse than a random distribution. In layman terms, this means a group of monkeys throwing darts at the stock tables would have performed at least as well.

Turning to market timing, Cowles tested the results of a strategy called Dow Theory, named after its founder, Charles Dow. The data gathered on Dow Theory actually followed the predictions of Dow's predecessor, William Peter Hamilton. From 1904 until his death in 1929, Hamilton wrote editorials in the Wall Street Journal where he made market predictions.

Hamilton made 90 separate market timing calls over the 26 year period. His results were a random event; 45 calls were right and 45 were wrong. This is the same result expected from flipping a coin.

Hamilton earned a total return of 12.0 percent per year over the 26 year period while the Dow Jones Industrial Average earned 15.5 percent per year. Corrections were made for the effect of brokerage commissions, dividends, and interest while Hamilton's funds were out of the market.

The Cowles Commission report failed to find any individual or organization with the ability to consistently select individual securities or foretell the market returns. Winning managers and analysts were consistent with chance rather than skill or insight, except for the worst forecasts, which appeared to be lower than expected by chance.

In summary, there are three consistencies to take away from active management:

1.Few active managers consistently outperform their benchmarks.

2.The winning managers do not outperform by much while the losing managers underperform by much more.

3.Past winning managers generally do not persist into the future. Thus, most outperformance is a result of luck rather than skill.

Wise investors don't rely on active management strategies to achieve their financial objectives, and there's no reason to anymore. Instead, allocate your assets for the long-term based on your financial need, and select low-cost index funds and ETFs to capture the returns of asset classes you select. A passive asset allocation strategy using low-cost index funds that is regularly maintained has the highest probability for reaching your financial goals.

APPENDIX NINE NEW INVESTORS

Most people that become interested in buying marketable securities come with preconceived notions on how to go about selecting stocks to buy for their portfolio. If you belong to this camp, and then you may find it difficult to accept what you will learn as you read this book. Believe me that diving into the market with your hard earned money without some understanding of how difficult and expensive it will be unless you first get some understanding about the market and the competition out there. There are hundreds and thousands of investors competing with you seeking to buy stocks that are undervalued to buy or overvalued to buy. At any instant in time the market as determined the correct price for each and every issue. Prices of securities change when some unanticipated event occurs and investors react to this random event.

APPENDIX TEN MARKET OUTLOOK FOR NEXT 30 YEARS

Using Gordon's formula over the next 30 years equities will return between 4% and 8% (real inflation adjusted returns). Bonds will return 2% real. The prices of equities and bonds will increase in value in step with inflation. At present the market is fairly priced with the S&P at 1100 for equities. Asset classes that are undervalued are the European market and real estate trusts (REIT).

The best equity allocation is 70% total domestic market and 30% foreign equities. And the debt allocation should be adjusted to your age. A 60 year old should have 60% debt and 40% equities.

If you need higher returns to retire tilt your portfolios toward value and small cap stocks for domestic equities and reduce bond allocation.

Owning a home is not an investment. When buying a home, offer 150 times the rental market. For example, a house that rents for $4,000 a month is worth $600,000. If the house you want costs less than $4,000 to rent then rent rather than purchase it

Long term returns on homes:

Luxury homes in Holland over last 400 years zero return after adjustment for inflation.

Domestic U.S. market 1890-1990 0% return inflation adjusted.

APPENDIX ELEVEN NATIONAL DEBT

The long-term economic health of the United States is threatened by $58 trillion in government debts and liabilities that start to come due in four years when baby boomers begin to retire.

The "Greatest Greatest Generation" and its baby-boom children have promised themselves benefits unprecedented in size and scope. Many leading economists say that even the world's most prosperous economy cannot fulfill these promises without a crushing increase in taxes — and perhaps not even then.

This hidden debt equals $473,456 per household, dwarfing the $84,454 each household owes in personal debt. The $58 trillion is what federal, state and local governments need immediately — stashed away, earning interest, beyond the $3 trillion in taxes collected last year — to repay debts and honor future benefits promised under Medicare, Social Security and government pensions. And like an unpaid credit card balance accumulating interest, the problem grows by more than $1 trillion every year that action to pay down the debt is delayed.

APPENDIX TWELVE PUBLIC SECTOR PENSIONS

In California, the cost of employing policeman or a fireman in Los Angeles is approximately $180,000 per year. That is for wages. The big costs occur when they stop working and retire at the age of 50 combined with inflation – linking, health benefits and lump sum payments for unused sick leave.

But California is also shelling out fortunes to retired state and municipal managers – more than 9,000 have retirement incomes of more than $100,000 per year. It has been estimated that the States

Unfunded pension liabilities are in the neighborhood of $574 billion and that they will have exhausted their pension assets within the next nine years. We see a conflict between public-sector employees and taxpayers, the majority of whom rely on social security and their personal savings, recently destroyed by the stock market crash. Social security itself is in big trouble and so is the so called "trust fund." The employee and worker contributions for the last 50 years never did exist, because it has been spent on the current government's costs. It is estimated that Congress has two choices: either increasing the age at which the benefits are paid or raising the contributions of the employer and workers to 30% of earned income, closing all of our military bases overseas, and declaring that we have won the wars in the Middle East.

Shortly, it will become obvious to the man on the street that our Congress is irresponsible when it comes to managing our tax dollars and that we are at the point that there is no solution to our problems except to renege on the promises the

Government has made to us all these years. The cure will be to change the way our government operates by a Constitutional amendment mandating term limits and reorganizing the way the committee system in Congress works. The public should demand that politicos be tried and punished in the same way that private citizens and when they steal and commit crimes.

APPENDIX THIRTEEN THE BIGGEST LIES

1.The total amount of all debt outstanding in the United States has increased from $25 trillion to over $60 trillion in just the last ten years, and this does not include the unfunded liabilities in Social Security and Medicare obligations. Over the last forty years, Congress, after stating that the money employees and their employers contributed to Social Security has been spent and that today all these funds, some 15% of earned wages have disappeared. We know that our legislators are not only liars but a bunch of thieves who cannot be trusted. Every one of the last 40 years, Congress has been told of this problem and the action it took was to increase the amount withheld by raising the earnings that would be taxed. Today, blue collar workers pay more in Social Security than they pay for income taxes. The money their employer pays is money that should have gone to the employees.

2.You will hear a lot of rhetoric to the effect that the employee will be receiving more money than he put into the plan, but if you count the interest that should have been earned over some 40 years, that is not a true statement.

3.Just as the Government has gone on a spending spree, so has the public by increasing credit card debt, and taking equity loans on their housing.

APPENDIX FOURTEEN VALUE AVERAGING

The investor sets a predetermined worth of the portfolio in each future time period, as a function of the size of the initial investment, the size of periodic investments and the yield expected. The investor then buys or sells sufficient shares of the investment such that the predetermined portfolio worth is achieved at each revalue averaging point. On revalue averaging timing, I suggest that, averaging quarterly is reasonable. In his own words, Edleson simply defines the value averaging concept: make the value averaging not (the market price) of your portfolio go up by a fixed amount each month." Considering movements in the investment's market price and the size of periodic investments, the investor then either acquires or disposes of sufficient units of the investment such that the investment's required value averaging is achieved at each subsequent revalue averaging point.

During periods of market price decline, the investor is required to purchase relatively many units to maintain portfolio value averaging. Conversely, during rising markets the technique requires the purchase of relatively few shares to achieve required value averaging. During these periods the extra money is put aside for those times that more shares are required to achieve the value-averaging target.

During extended bull markets or during unusually large upward spikes in market price, the technique requires that units be sold to maintain portfolio value averaging at the desired level. This technique is even more intuitively appealing than dollar cost averaging. As with dollar cost averaging, more investment units are purchased when prices are low. However, value averaging requires that relatively more units be purchased as prices decline than does dollar cost averaging since the unit price decline reduces the value averaging of the portfolio. Furthermore, and contrary to dollar cost averaging, value averaging gives a rule for selling. As the market price increases, beyond what it was recently, value averaging may require unit sales since the growing price rise increases the value averaging of the portfolio. And, if the market price continues to increase dramatically, value averaging gives even more aggressive sell signals to control the value averaging of the portfolio to the level desired.

Intuitively, DOLLAR COST AVERAGING is contrary in the sense that fewer shares are purchased when price are 'high' and more shares are purchased when price are 'low', facilitating the 'buy- low' aspect of the ancient investment adage, 'buy low, sell high.'" VALUE AVERAGING conceptually does an even better job. Even more units are purchased at "low" prices and probably some, at least, are sold at "high" prices. The American Association of Individual investors (AAII) follows VALUE AVERAGING closely. One should consider joining the organization if you intend to follow the method. AAII claims an historical increase of returns of 1 ½%.

APPENDIX FIFTEEN SORTINO RATIO

This ratio is computationally very similar to the Sharpe Ratio, but divides from the excess return of the portfolio by the standard deviation of the negative returns. The Sortino Ratio therefore uses downside standard deviation as the proxy for risk for investors, instead of using standard deviation of all the fund's returns, as this number includes upside standard deviation. This in effect removes the negative penalty that the Sharpe Ratio imposes on positive returns.

To help you intuitively use this ratio, imagine a hypothetical portfolio, Portfolio A, which never experiences negative returns. However, Portfolio A has incredible standard deviation in its positive returns: one day it returns 0.1% and another 1000%. The standard deviation of Portfolio A will therefore be very large. When measured by Sharpe Ratio, Portfolio A will have a low ratio, because it is symmetric in its treatment of upside and downside deviation. However, the Sortino Ratio of Portfolio A will be infinite! This is the case because there is zero standard deviation in negative returns. The Sortino Ratio only considers downside standard deviation as important.

Similarly, imagine Portfolio B, where there are only negative returns. In this case, the Sharpe Ratio and the Sortino Ratio will be exactly the same. Therefore, the higher the Sortino Ratio, the better the risk adjusted (as measured by downside standard deviation) returns are for your portfolio.

APPENDIX SIXTEEN FINANCIAL FACTS

Full service stockbrokers do not have a fiduciary duty to supply their customers with financial products that are suitable for them considering their age, net worth and skill in using financial products. These brokers live and work in a culture where the client is a helpless sheep waiting patiently to be sheered. The broker is compensated and rewarded when he sells and promotes toxic financial products. These rewards include paid vacation trips, bonuses for selling certain products and other perks.

Insurance agents are permitted under law to promote and sell equity-indexed annuities. This toxic product is sold with a guarantee that the investor will receive a guaranteed 8% return on his investment. This is an outright falsehood. Currently insurance companies have difficulty meeting their obligations on some insurance products that have a true 3% return.

The indexed annuity is sold using some math that uses an 8% multiplier but, in reality, the actual earnings rate of the deferred annuity is about .2%, that's two tenths of one percent. The agent will not let you take the contract to study or show to a competent third party but presses you for a signature now with a time period to cancel the contract. The surrender fees are in the nature of 14%. This product carries the highest commission that an insurance agent can earn. That free lunch that you get for attending a sales meeting will be the most expensive meal you will ever eat.

With respect to stocks and bonds one should be careful that for the level of risk you take that you are adequately compensated for taking that risk. That makes sense does it not? Uncompensated risk can be virtually eliminated with a portfolio of a large number of stocks. To virtually eliminate uncompensated risk for domestic stocks a portfolio of about 3,500 different securities is required.

Other things to look for are: low expense ratios, low portfolio turnover, compound annual returns, not average annual return. Knowing the portfolios standard deviation will enable you to compute the compound annual return but the mutual fund salesman will not voluntary give you that number if indeed he knows what the term means.

Be aware that a properly constructed portfolio of securities will produce a return significantly higher return than the weighted average return of its individual components. If your broker doesn't know what you are talking about find another broker.

Be aware that even highly talented and highly compensated professional portfolio managers have difficulty meeting the return of the total domestic stock market after the costs and fees they incur trying to beat the market. In fact it is extremely difficult if not impossible to separate those managers that have skill from those who were just lucky.

There are a number of data items that should be required so investors can evaluate when purchasing securities specifically mutual funds. They are:

- Portfolio turnover for 3,5, and 10 year periods
- Compound returns for 3,5, and 10-year periods.
- Risk compared to the total stock market for the comparable periods.

There are some long-term problems on the horizon that are caused by demographic trends that need attention. The latest crisis originated from the baby boom from returning servicemen from the Second World War. When the baby boomers reached maturity we had a housing boom, which together with the expansion of credit caused a business boom that was based on financing of housing and the availability of equity and credit card financing. This boom was financed by loans that were beyond the ability of the borrowers to repay.

A recession caused by excessive credit card debt and loans on household equity loans is very difficult to manage because a financial stimulus is not effective.

Now currently the population is aging and simultaneously the birthrate is falling. This means relatively fewer workers with an expanding senior population. This means inflation coupled with rising prices due to the shift between workers and retirees. Add to this the problem of the defined benefit pensions of public service employees and the defined contribution pension plans of private industry.

There is a world of difference between these two methods of income for retirees. The public service employees are recipients of guaranteed pensions often contain inflation indexing for inflation and medical benefits and defined contribution plans offered by private industry that shifts risk from the company to the employee who by no stretch of the imagination is capable of handling the risk factors.

The typical worker is not capable of reading and understanding the factors required to managing a portfolio of securities and the fees for professional portfolio managers are prohibitive.

Now for the really bad and discouraging part. Our political system is blatantly corrupt when it comes to regulating the financial system. First, the employees of the government in our regulatory system are outmatched by the employees of the financial services industry.

Lobbyists are able to grease the chairmen of the important committees to the extent that the funds available to virtually guarantee their re-election. The financial services industry could dig up FDR and run him for reelection and win for example with lobby funds available.

APPENDIX SEVENTEEN BYPASS TRUSTS

Of course, a married person may leave an unlimited amount of assets to his or her spouse, free of estate taxes and without using up any of the estate tax credit. The problem is that if the second spouse then dies with an estate worth more than the exempted amount, his or her estate would be subject to estate tax. Meanwhile, the first spouse's estate tax credit was unused and, in effect, wasted.

The bypass trust was created to take care of this problem. This type of trust may be revocable or irrevocable, and living or testamentary. Typically, the trust instrument initially creates a single living trust that is revocable.

Upon the death of the first spouse, the instrument establishes a separate, irrevocable "bypass" trust with the deceased spouse's share of the trust's assets. The surviving spouse is the beneficiary of this trust, with the children as beneficiaries of the remaining interest.

The irrevocable trust is funded to the extent of the first spouse's exemption. Thus, the amount in the irrevocable trust is not subject to estate taxes on the death of the first spouse, and the trust takes full advantage of the first spouse's estate tax credit.

At the same time, special language is used in the irrevocable trust so that the assets in the irrevocable trust will not be included in the taxable estate of the beneficiary (i.e., the other spouse). Generally this involves giving the second spouse only limited powers to control the trust assets. Thus, the bypass trust is aptly named, as the assets in the irrevocable trust "bypass" the estate tax that would be assessed when the second spouse dies.

APPENDIX EIGHTEEN EQUITY/FIXED INCOME ALLOCATION 38

Turning to ABILITY, this relates to your ability to withstand the ups and downs of the market without getting nervous and making changes to your asset allocation. Selling in the face of a decline is about the worst thing you can do. Here is a table offered by author Larry Swedroe, based on the 1970s bear market, showing the amount of decline for various stock/bond allocations:

Max Equity - Exposure Max loss

Max Equity - Exposure	Max loss
20%	5%
30%	10%
40%	15%
50%	20%
60%	25%
70%	30%
80%	35%
90%	40%
100%	50%

There are other ways to determine an asset allocation, including several rules of thumb:

• Your age in bonds. So, if you are 40 years old, then use a 60/40 (equity/bond) allocation.

• 110 minus your age = equities (110-40 yrs old=70/30 asset allocation)

• 120 minus your age = equities (120-40 yrs old = 80/20 asset allocation)

BIBLIOGRAPHY

Finding a good book to read about investing is a harder task than trying to make money by speculating in stocks. So here is a selection of the very good books to read.

The Loser's Game. This is the book that I found and started me using index funds. I didn't buy the book – it was a gift from Charles Ellis when he attended a talk I was giving on our company that had just floated a secondary offering and I was making the traditional pep talk a company makes to the broker that will sell the stock in the offering. Charley asked for my card and I received his book shortly later in the mail. Charley is a on the staff of the executive branch of our government in Washington the last I heard.

The Bogleheads' Guide to Investing by Taylor Larimore, Mel Lindauer, and Michael LeBoeuf

Common Sense on Mutual Funds by John C. Bogle

All About Asset Allocation by Richard A, Ferri

All About Index Funds by Richard A. Ferri

Protecting Your Wealth in Good Times and Bad by Richard A. Ferri

The Intelligent Asset Allocator by William Bernstein

Index Mutual Funds by W.Scott Simon

Rational Investing in Irrational Times by Larry E. Swedroe

Winning the Loser's Game by Charles D. Ellis

The Exchange Traded Funds Manual by Gary I. Gastineau

The Informed Investor by Frank Armstrong III

A Random Walk Down Wall Street by Burton G. Malkiel

Winning Investment Strategy by Larry E. Swedroe
Exchange Traded Funds by Jim Wiandt & Will McClatchy
The Four Pillars of Investing by William Bernstein
Rational Investing in Irrational Times by Larry
E. Swedroe. I have all of Larry's books in my library. He has read the book you are reading and has verified the accuracy of the facts. Larry's books are easy to read and crystal clear. His latest book is a winner.

The Bogleheads' Guide to Investing by Taylor Larimore, Mel Lindauer, and Michael LeBoeuf

Three authors for the price of one.

Be sure and go to the Boglehead's Web site for up to the minute information on investing and any other subject.

We all are indebted to Mr. Bogle for founding Vanguard.

I am sure that the 19,000,000 shareholders of Vanguard funds will agree to the following statement. "Thank you Mr. Bogle for creating this wonderful company that the shareholders of Vanguard funds own."

Mr. Bogle likes to be called Jack. He is my age now 84, but says he is 36 because several years ago he had a new heart put in and the donor was 36 years old. Jack has written several books and I suspect he has someone on the staff of Vanguard help.

Common Sense on Mutual Funds by John C. Bogle

If you need someone to help with your investments I highly recommend Rick Ferri. His books are among the best and for those of you who need an advisor I recommend Rick Ferri. When I pass away and go to the happy hunting ground my account goes to Rick to manage. His fees are the lowest in the industry, only one half of 1%. Here are some of Rick's books:

The EFT Book All You Need to About Exchange Traded Funds by Richard A. Ferri

Rick's latest books is: *The Power of Passive Investing: More Wealth with Less Work* (Hardcover - Dec 7, 2010)

The following author is a genius and a regular warehouse of information. This book is a little advanced for the beginner but you will eventually buy the book. I did.

The Intelligent Asset Allocator by William Bernstein

Now the next book by Bernstein is a lesson in the history of investing going way back thousands of years. You will learn about risk using simple and direct examples.

Bill's next book I recommend is very readable,. interesting, and useful. The title is *The Birth of Plenty: How the Prosperity of the Modern World was Created.* If you have never taken a course in Economic history as I have here is your opportunity to have a master of the English language spoon feed you economics. The book is a joy to read. The book is brilliantly written, a fast moving journey through the history of investing money throughout the world. I am sending my copy to my Senator to read and to influence his vote on the floor of the Senate.

Now, if you have been taken for several million dollars or your company or your employees here is the guy to hire. Simon is a securities lawyer whose practice is getting justice in court on security issues. He book reads like a lawyers brief and discloses risks and rewards clearly. The book gives you a bibliography that he uses in some of the law suites used in his practice, my son is a securities lawyer and knows of his practice.

Index Mutual Funds by W. Scott Simon

Value Averaging by Michael l E. Edleson

The Informed Investor by Frank Armstrong III

What Wall Street doesn't Want You to Know
    Protecting Your Wealth in Good Times and Bad
    By Richard A, Ferri
    The Four Pillars of Investing by William Bernstein
    The investor's manifesto preparing for prosperity, Armageddon, and everything in between by William J, Bernstein

Your Money and Your Brain. How the New Science of Neuroeconomics can help you get rich By Jason Zweig

Jason is a financial writer originally with *Money Magazine,* a periodical that you can trust. Just last year Jason moved to the Wall Street Journal a career promotion. We hope he takes with him his scholarship, honesty and concern for the small investor and improve the material printed by the Journal.

Jason shows you how your mind is tricked what you read, what you see on financial TV and gives you a short course on the new science of Neuroeconomics. Like Jason I had a brain scan to check the arteries in my brain.

WEB REFERENCE & RESEARCH SITES

www.Morningstar.com[1]

On this website, you will find conversations among investors who follow the strategies I recommend. Go to the box titled Discuss and click on Diehards. There are about 375,000 postings in these conversations.

www.moneychimp.com[2]

On this website, you will find a wealth of information from portfolio theory to sophisticated computer simulations to discover within limits how long your retirement savings will last.

www.vanguard.com[3]

This is the official website for the Vanguard Group. Here you can find detailed descriptions and up to date data on every Vanguard Index Fund as well as their actively managed Mutual Funds.

http://www.altruistfa.com/readingroomarticles.htm

At this website you will find hundreds of articles on finance and investments that are of interest to those who wish to fine tune their portfolios and keep abreast of developments.

www.Lostsprings.com/diehards/chapters[4]

At this web site you will find the location and schedule of a group of investors who follow passive investing techniques us-

---

1.   http://www.Morningstar.com

2.   http://www.moneychimp.com

3. http://www.vanguard.com

4.   http://www.Lostsprings.com/diehards/chapters

ing Vanguard low cost index funds. These investors meet periodically at local chapters throughout the country. At these meetings you will meet other investors eager to help you with your investment program and to supply you with support during those uncomfortable periods when the market crashes for no reason at all, which it will surely do a couple times during your accumulation phase.

CNN Students News www.cnnfyi.com[5]

U.S. and World news multimedia tailored to the needs of students.

Conversion Tables www.convert-me.com[6]

Convert length, area, speed, temperature, etc., into different units and systems.

eLibrary Research: www.elibrary[7].com

Search any topic using a data base of current newspapers, magazines, books and more.

Encyclopedia Britannica : www.briticannica.com[8]

On line version of one of the world's most trusted sources of information on every topic imaginable.

Fact Monster: www.factmonster.com[9] Designed for kids of all ages, this site offers an amazing array of facts and figures in addition to homework help, an almanac, dictionary and much more.

Gallup Organization: www.gallop.com[10]

---

5.   http://www.cnnfyi.com

6.   http://www.convert-me.com

7.   http://www.elibrary

8.   http://www.briticannica.com

9.   http://www.factmonster.com

10.   http://www.gallop.com

Search thousands of poll results, special reports, societal trends and social audits.

Hoovers Business Research: www.hoovers.com[11]

Comprehensive index of over 45,000 leading U.S. private and public companies.

Information Please Almanac: www.infoplease.com[12]

Online almanac offering millions of interesting and useful facts on a wide variety of subjects.

Internet Public Library : www.ipl.org[13]

An exhausting collection of over 20,000 titles.

iTools Research: www.itools.com[14]

Collection of online research tools including dictionaries, translations, quotations and more.

Library of Congress: www.loc.gov[15]

Easy to use reference catalog for accessing the collections of the Library of Congress.

National Archives: www.archives.gov[16]

National Archives online directory of U.S. Federal records.

Smithsonian Institution: www.si.edu[17]

User-friendly site from the world's largest museum complex and research organization.

U.S. Census Bureau: www.census.gov[18]

---

11.   http://www.hoovers.com

12.   http://www.infoplease.com

13.   http://www.ipl.org

14.   http://www.itools.com

15.   http://www.loc.gov

16.   http://www.archives.gov

17.   http://www.si.edu

18.   http://www.census.gov

A wealth of basic information about the U.S .broken down on a national, state and local level.

U.S. Federal Government : www.fedstats.gov[19] Statistical information from over 100 federal agencies.

U.S. Department of Labor: http://bls.gov

Bureau of Labor statistics site containing labor statistics and links to hundreds of state and federal agencies.

OTHER BOOKS BY KENNETH EADE

Brent Marks Legal Thriller Series

A Patriot's Act

Predatory Kill

HOA Wire

Unreasonable Force

Killer.com

Absolute Intolerance

The Spy Files

Decree of Finality

Beyond All Recognition

The Big Spill

And Justice?

Involuntary Spy Espionage Series

An Involuntary Spy
To Russia for Love

Stand Alone

Terror on Wall Street

Paladine Political Thriller Series

Paladine
Russian Holiday
Traffick Stop
Unwanted

ABOUT THE AUTHORS

Described by critics as "one of our strongest thriller writers on the scene," author Kenneth Eade, best known for his legal and political thrillers, practiced International law, Intellectual Property law and E-Commerce law for 30 years before publishing his first novel, "An Involuntary Spy." Eade, an award-winning, best-selling Top 100 thriller author, has been described by his peers as "one of the up-and-coming legal thriller writers of this generation." He is the 2015 winner of Best Legal Thriller from Beverly Hills Book Awards and the 2016 winner of a bronze medal in the category of Fiction, Mystery and Murder from the Reader's Favorite International Book Awards. His latest novel, "Paladine," a quarter-finalist in Publisher's Weekly's

2016 BookLife Prize for Fiction and finalist in the 2017 RONE Awards. Eade has authored three fiction series: The "Brent Marks Legal Thriller Series", the "Involuntary Spy Espionage Series" and the "Paladine Anti-Terrorism Series." He has written eighteen novels which have been translated into French, Spanish, Italian and Portuguese.

Gordon L. Eade is a retired author, with a background in business administration and accounting. Gordon worked for Union bank, for Gulf oil, for U.S. Borax, for Litton Industries, for the government of Greece, and for Daniel, Mann & Johnson, in various capacities as engineer, accounting system designer, and tourist and industrial development executive, over the years. Gordon's books and articles on finance and how to make money in the stock market are critically acclaimed.

This publication is designed to provide accurate and authoritative information in regard to the subject matter covered. It is sold with the understanding that the publisher is not engaged in rendering legal, accounting, or other professional services. If you require legal advice or other professional assistance; you should seek the services of a competent individual. Investing in stocks, bonds, and derivative products requires the assumption risks not easily understood by the average investor. You are cautioned that you must not engage in speculative activities until you thoroughly understand the risks involved. Further, it is imperative that you understand that when you take on a risk you may or may not receive the appropriative expected return for the risk taken. You are cautioned that in no other activity are there are so many scam artists that are extremely skilled in taking your money and leaving you broke and destitute. Some of these villains work for our largest and most highly respected firms.